TAX FREEZE

How to File & Win Property Tax Appeals in Georgia!

Matthew S. Chan

Ascend Beyond Publishing

TAX FREEZE
How to File & Win Property Tax Appeals in Georgia!

ISBN-13 (Print): 978-1-933723-09-9

Matthew Chan, MBA
Real Estate Broker/Instructor
Georgia R.E. License: #391253
Georgia R.E. Instructor: #435531
Email: MattRealty1@gmail.com

http://TaxFreezeCommand.com

Kindle Book edition
Version 1.0 April 30, 2023
Version 1.01 December 15, 2023
Version 2.0 April 8, 2025
Version 2.01 June 1, 2026

Print Book edition
Version 1.0 December 15, 2023
Version 2.0 April 8, 2025
Version 2.01 June 1, 2026

Publisher: Ascend Beyond Publishing

For Susan:

Without her love and support, this book and my other projects would not be possible.

*****

For Tony:

Thank you for inspiring me to publish the print version of this book.

*****

CONTENTS

DISCLAIMER

This book is meant for general education and general information purposes only. It is nowhere close to expert advice for your individual situation. You are not my client. You are a book customer.

I've done my best to get my information right in this book but you bear responsibility to verify and corroborate any information anyone provides you.

I am not a real estate appraiser. I cannot discuss property valuation in the sophisticated way a real estate appraiser can. I discuss property valuation in a simpler (and occasionally simplistic) manner than most real estate appraisers would.

I am not a lawyer. I am not giving any legal advice but I do offer personal opinions on legal matters for informational purposes. My opinion is nowhere close to being expert legal advice to anyone's situation.

There are 159 counties in Georgia. As such, there are 159 tax assessor offices. I do not have direct experience with all 159 Georgia counties. Every tax assessor office has their own customs and way of doing things although all of them are supposed to follow the same Georgia laws that regulate property tax appeals in Georgia.

This book is focused on residential property with a big emphasis on homeowners and landlords appealing single-family homes.

However, a lot of what I write in this book can be applied to other types of properties. There are many additional issues and nuances I can't cover in this book.

Last thing, if you ordered this book through the Amazon Kindle eBook platform, you will receive free updates and revisions. As

I get new information and feedback, I will update this book with the latest information and insights. It is a free benefit for being an Amazon Kindle customer.

2025 UPDATE

In 2024, Georgia's H.B. 581 was passed and went into effect January 1, 2025. The full effect and impact of H.B. 581 on Georgia's tax appeals is uncertain as I go to print.

A portion of H.B. 581 makes minor changes to Georgia's property tax appeal system. However, what is supposed to happen and what will actually happen remains to be seen. We will find out together beginning with the 2025 Georgia tax appeal season.

I've made updates to this book to reflect my latest experiences with the tax appeal process and changes enacted in H.B. 581. However, as always, you bear sole responsibility to check and verify with your local tax assessors office ANY changes or modifications with the tax appeal process.

Visit my YouTube channel "Tax Freeze Command" at http://youtube.com/@TaxFreezeCommand.

Visit my website GeorgiaTaxAppealInfo.com for the latest updates.

PREFACE

In 2009-2010 during the Great Recession, I found myself in a financially difficult situation. Credit had dried up, real estate values plunged, unemployment was up, and our tenant-buyers did not have the money to pay nor were they interested in lease-optioning properties we offered. My business partner and I were forced into less-profitable traditional rentals to keep our properties occupied.

As anyone experienced in traditional rentals know, the margins can be thin and even non-existent if there is substantial vacancy, turnover, and deferred maintenance.

During this time, we couldn't increase rents and we couldn't collect more security deposits but we had many mortgages that we had to pay month after month. These mortgages felt relentless and crushing without sufficient cash and credit reserves to fall back on to carry us over through tough times.

It was during this time I was looking to cut costs and trim the fat wherever I could. Within our mortgage payments, I knew there were principal, interest, taxes, and insurance (aka P.I.T.I). I knew I could not change the principal and interest. They were on a fixed amortization schedule. However, I did have some control and influence over taxes and insurance.

I went on an aggressive campaign of mortgage cost-cutting and evaluated every property insurance policy we had. I changed them from replacement-cost policies to "actual cash value" (ACV) policies. We were able to slash our premiums significantly which, in turn, would lower the escrow portion of our mortgage payments.

I previously heard of property tax appeals. But like so many property owners, I really didn't want to learn about it and I was intimidated by the thought of it.

But because of our dire financial situation and my instinct to fight for financial survival, I made phone calls and visited our local tax assessors office for the first time.

It was there I was directed to the county's tax appeal form with basic instructions to fill out the form. It wasn't just one form I had to fill out, I had many forms to fill out, one for each property, because we owned and managed several properties.

Through sheer repetition, I learned my first lessons of how to initiate a property tax appeal. What I submitted to the tax assessors office was largely a stack of barebone forms and perhaps a few muddled attachments at best.

After I submitted the stack of appeal forms, I simply waited for the process to unfold. I would periodically call into our tax assessors office to find out what the next steps were. As every notice came in, I would follow-up and respond the best I could.

I found that nearly every appeal I submitted came back with a value reduction which I was thrilled. I realized I scored some early wins by simply filling out the form. There were others that had no adjustment or an adjusted value that was unsatisfactory to me.

In those cases, I waited for the next steps which was supposed to be the Board of Equalization (BOE) hearings. However, for many years, I never attended BOE hearings because I learned that the county appraisers (at that time) would reach out to property owners and propose a settlement with a better value.

Again, I was thrilled with the results. I was getting lower values (which meant lower property tax bills) and I did not have to attend any BOE hearing.

It was during this time that I successfully stumbled my way through the property tax appeal process (securing "tax freezes" along the way) did I fully realize I should have done all this much sooner.

Months later, the annual mortgage escrow statements from our various properties started coming with with big escrow refunds and, more importantly, lower mortgage payments. We had never experienced this before because we rarely shopped our insurance. And we never filed property tax appeals before.

It would be a few more years and a couple dozen tax appeals later that I began to slowly share my knowledge with a couple of real estate investor friends about the benefits of going through the property tax appeal process.

However, it was 2017 where I had my biggest year- to-date. I filed 65 property tax appeals across three Georgia counties for numerous property owners. There were so many properties to track, I had to create a spreadsheet and filing system to track the 65 tax appeals. I had several discussions with tax assessor offices and the BOEs during this time.

When all 65 tax appeals were completed in early 2018, I had learned so much and internalized the entire property tax appeal process that I began putting together information to help others.

Today, I have since produced numerous YouTube videos for people to learn from. You can find my videos about property tax appeals on my "Tax Freeze Command" YouTube channel.

http://youtube.com/@TaxFreezeCommand

I also teach real estate agents and property owners how to file property tax appeals for themselves and their clients.

Through my growing network of friends, associates, and clients and their properties, I have been able to gain insights into how different Georgia counties and their tax assessor office operate.

In turn, I share my information and insights with you so that property owners can be educated and empowered on the subject.

INTRODUCTION

As an independent publisher and author, I am not beholden to anyone. I can write anything I want, however I want. Although this is generally an informational and educational book on a relatively obscure topic, I have intentionally woven in personal opinions and commentary to an otherwise dry book.

I say this because this book is not designed to be an objective textbook or instruction manual. It is meant to be a starting point for education and dialog.

This book is not meant to be the end-all, be-all on the subject of Georgia property tax appeals. There is always room in this book for improvement but I have to start somewhere.

I wrote this book because, as of this writing, no one has written or published a book on Amazon (or anywhere I could find) to educate the general public on the subject of Georgia property tax appeals. I have undertaken this project under the umbrella as publisher and a real estate broker/adviser/instructor. It is a way for me to help, serve, and reach those that I cannot meet.

I do my best to get it right but I occasionally make educated guesses or speculate as to how tax assessor offices (TAOs) operate behind the scenes because very few are willing to open up and discuss how they truly think and operate. My instinct tells me that many of us would not be happy to see how the sausage is made.

Government agencies like TAOs are populated by people. And people are imperfect. Most TAOs are under scrutiny and political pressures in addition to the normal pressures associated with working in any larger organization. They are frequently attacked and insulted by the citizens they serve. So, it is not an easy job they do.

Unfortunately, they are also our financial adversaries if they attempt to persuade us to go along with tax assessments that are unjustifiable or unsubstantiated. Their assessments directly impact the taxes property owners have to pay.

I don't hide the fact that I believe we should not have to pay any more taxes than we should. I don't believe property owners are obligated to pay more taxes "just to be nice".

At the same time, I understand that tax assessments are a tricky thing. They are based as much on people's opinions, not just data from mass appraisals and actual sales.

TAOs purport to follow state law in their job. Unfortunately, I have seen the same laws executed very differently from county to county or even within the same office.

I have learned that what they do is both imperfect and flawed. The sausage that we call "property assessments" and "property tax appeals" culminate in a collective county tax roll reported to the Georgia Department of Revenue every year.

The people most victimized by this highly-flawed, sausage-making process are property owners who never participate. They turn a blind eye year after year. They pay no regard to their annual assessment notices and blindly pay their property tax bills because they are uninformed, cannot be bothered, or they are too intimidated by it.

I decided that I want to help those that do care about their property taxes and willing to learn how to stand up for themselves. If you are reading this book, you are among this tiny minority.

You care enough to be informed and that matters to me. In that spirit, I feel the need to give you more than just the nuts and bolts or be an objective textbook.

I have been in business for nearly 30 years and have life experiences that come from many places. I bring everything I know: my education, my research, my professional experiences, my knowledge, and my instincts into any project I take on. Taking on property tax assessments and property tax appeals is no different.

When you read this book, I've done my best to separate facts from opinions. But remember, there are 159 counties in Georgia. Each county has a tax assessors office operated by imperfect human beings vulnerable to self-serving interests and subject to influences and pressures from others. And each county does things their way. Beware.

ABBREVIATED TERMS

In this book, I will occasionally abbreviate certain phrases and terms for readability purposes.

"Annual Notice of Assessment" will occasionally be referred to as "assessment notice", "notice of assessment", "annual notice", or "PT-306".

"Board of Equalization" will occasionally be abbreviated "BOE".

"Board of Tax Assessors" will occasionally be abbreviated "BTA".

"Fair Market Value" or "Market Value" will occasionally be abbreviated "FMV".

"Letter of Authorization" will occasionally be abbreviated "LOA".

"Property tax appeal" will be sometimes be abbreviated to "tax appeal". In this book, we are not discussing any other forms of taxes except property taxes unless otherwise specified.

"Tax Assessors Office" or "Tax Assessment Office" will occasionally be abbreviated as "TAO" or "TAOs" (plural). Some counties may refer to their tax assessment office as Property Appraisal department or Property Assessment department. In this book, I will refer to all these name variations as "tax assessors office", "TAO", or "TAOs".

CHAPTER 1: BEWARE LOCAL CUSTOMS

As of the publication of this book, I've had direct dealings and interactions with six different Georgia county tax assessor offices (TAOs) so far. (I expect this number will grow over time.) That means I have either filed a property tax appeal on my own properties, another person's property, or I was an agent for someone's property tax appeal.

What I have found frustrating, which I always warn people about, is that every TAO has their own local customs of implementing and executing the same Georgia laws regarding tax appeals.

If you deal with a TAO long enough, you will inevitably hear that "their way" is "following Georgia law" which is an insinuation that "their way" is the "right way" to be compliant with Georgia law. (This is not always true.)

For 20 years, as a property owner, property manager, and landlord, I filed evictions in a city that had two different small claims courts: municipal court and magistrate court. The paperwork, the eviction process, and fees for each court were very different.

Court clerks from each court would say they were following Georgia law. And each group of court clerks would largely be oblivious to how the "other" small court operated when it came to evicting tenants.

As a private citizen interacting and communicating with both courts, I was being told different things.

It was generally pointless to discuss the differences with the court clerks because all they knew (and all they cared about) was the court office they worked in.

Similarly, this happens with each TAO I've dealt with. So far, I have dealt with six different TAOs in Georgia and each one is very different. Of course, there are similarities because they are legally required to follow the basic framework and umbrella of Georgia law as it relates to property tax appeals. But I can promise you that every TAO has their own "personality", "their way," and local customs when handling property tax appeals.

At every TAO, I find that lower-level clerks are largely oblivious to the customs or even the existence of other TAOs. Most lower-level clerks are hourly employees with a limited scope in their jobs. I don't fault them for it because they generally have large workloads especially in the larger counties.

I find that there is a fair amount of turnover in those front-line positions. When I communicate with higher managers of a TAO, there is a greater awareness of the existence of other TAOs. There is a recognition that different TAOs operate differently from one county to another. You can sometimes have meaningful and insightful conversations with them.

I say all this so you are better prepared in dealing with any TAO. If you are put into the position of dealing with more than one TAO at a time (especially if you are filing appeals on multiple properties located in different counties), you should not automatically assume that what you do correctly in one county will be fully accepted in another.

And sometimes even when you are dealing with the same TAO, you get different responses when dealing with different employees. You can even deal with the same TAO but then they change how they do things now compared to prior years.

These are all things that have happened to me. I am passing this on to you. Stay sharp, stay open, stay prepared.

CHAPTER 2: THE ANNUAL NOTICE OF ASSESSMENT

> GEORGIA ANNUAL NOTICE OF ASSESSMENT (PT-306)

Every year, an "Annual Notice of Assessment" is generated for all properties and parcels in Georgia. This Annual Notice of Assessment is formally known in Georgia as the PT-306 Form.

In this book, for the sake of brevity, I occasionally refer to "Annual Notice of Assessment" as "assessment notice" or "PT-306".

There are 159 counties in Georgia. Each county assesses properties and parcels within their county line. For example, if you own or manage more than one property in multiple counties, you should expect to receive assessment notices from different counties.

Because I own, manage, and assist property owners with their property tax appeals every year, I see assessment notices from multiple counties each year. I track 15 Georgia counties in a spreadsheet. So I have a good idea when each county will release and mail out their assessment notices every year.

For example, Gwinnett County in northeast metro Atlanta is an "early" county. They generally mail out their assessment notices mid-to-late April. Fulton County at the heart of metro Atlanta is a "late" county. They generally mail out their assessment notices in late June. However, the majority of Georgia counties I track and follow release their assessment notices in the May timeframe.

Depending on where your properties are located in Georgia, you can expect to see assessment notices anywhere from mid-April to late June. It is your job to find out when you can expect to receive your assessment notices in the mail.

However, for property owners who have not paid attention to their prior annual assessment notices, it is not uncommon for these notices to be lost in the mail or never delivered because of outdated mailing address information or clerical errors in the mailing address.

No matter the reason, the county's position is that every property owner has the responsibility to inform their TAO of any mailing address changes or corrections.

If your TAO does not have the correct mailing address for your property or parcel, sometimes you can call them over the phone and they will correct it on the spot. More often though, you will have to visit the TAO in person, submit an email, or write a short note to the TAO to correct the mailing address for future annual assessment notices.

Although you are not required to have the annual assessment notice in hand, almost all the information you need to file your property tax appeal is on that form.

Because of the importance of the PT-306 assessment notice, I consider it Step 1 on the road to filing your property tax appeal.

> WHAT IF YOU DON'T HAVE YOUR ASSESSMENT NOTICE?

If you didn't receive your annual assessment notice, the first thing you should do is call your TAO and ask if the annual assessment notices have been mailed out. If they have been mailed out, ask when they mailed it so you can determine if the notice is in the mail enroute to you.

Even with today's slower U.S. Mail service, it should take no more than a week to receive your annual assessment notice in the mail. Something has gone wrong if the assessment notice doesn't show up in one week.

Generally, each TAO mails out annual assessment notices around the same time frame every year but that is only a guideline, not a specific rule. If you call the TAO, they should be able to give you more specific information or at least a good estimation of when you should receive your assessment notice.

If you are on the phone with the TAO, you should ask what mailing address they have on record for each property you expect to receive an assessment notice. I have seen situations where there is a correct mailing address on one assessment notice but incorrect on another. It happens for various reasons. Regardless of reason, it needs to be corrected as soon as possible.

If everything checks out, you have waited a sufficient amount of time, and you still don't have your assessment notice, most larger counties have a website that will allow you to download a PDF copy of your assessment notice.

For those counties that provide that service, it is very convenient. In some counties, you can even download a copy of your neighbors' assessment notices for research and comparison purposes.

But for those counties that don't provide these online capabilities, ask the TAO to email you or FAX a copy to you.

> BREAKDOWN OF THE PT-306 ASSESSMENT NOTICE

There are several pieces of information on the PT-306 that every property should pay attention to and become familiar with when they receive their assessment notice.

UPPER SECTION

Tax assessment authority information: This is the tax assessor office you will engage and communicate with regarding your property tax appeal. The official mailing address and phone number is provided here.

Property owner name and mailing address: Is it correct? If not, you will want to correct this as soon as possible for future notices and letters.

The annual assessment notice date: This is very important because it is the official date of the assessment notice. It is also the date from which the 45-day tax appeal deadline date is calculated.

Last date to file a written appeal: This date should be 45 calendar days after the office annual assessment notice. It is the deadline for you to file your tax appeal with the tax assessors office.

MIDDLE SECTION

Property ID Number: This is sometimes known as the Parcel ID. This the unique identifier for your property. You will use this unique identifier for your tax appeal. The TAO will frequently ask for or refer to this unique identifier instead of street address to prevent confusion with another property with a similar street address name.

Homestead: If this is your primary residence, you want to make sure the box says "YES". If it does not, you will want to apply for Homestead exemption by April of the following year.

Property Address: This is the address you are most likely to recognize and how most citizens refer to an individual property.

100% Appraised Value: You most want to pay attention to Current Year Fair Market Value. This is the value that will be used to calculate property taxes you owe for that tax year. It is also the value that is most often incorrect. It causes property owners to overpay property taxes. Most of this book is focused on appealing, negotiating, and adjusting this value.

> WHY ASSESSMENT NOTICES ARE WRONG

The reason why most assessment notices are wrong is due to the imperfect nature of mass appraisal systems. There is no practical or cost-effective way to assess every property in a county individually or by hand without using a mass appraisal system. The number of properties and parcels in any given county can number in the tens or even hundreds of thousands.

In simplistic terms, a mass appraisal system is a software-based system that contain many inputs (such as number of bedrooms, bathrooms, square footage, etc.), market data (such as market sales values and sales dates), other internal calculations or adjustments, and manual adjustments (property defects, damage, deficiencies, etc.) which then outputs an "assessed value".

This assessed value on the assessment notice is a calculation and estimation of fair market value (FMV) based on the determination of a mass appraisal software system. It is, at best, a ballpark number of the value of your property.

It is nowhere close to a formal appraisal where a property is carefully scrutinized and evaluated down to individual fixtures, appliances, and other individual property characteristics.

Another basic reason why most assessment notices are wrong for residential single-family homes is that market sales information that is compiled and collected are generally based on retail-ready, fixed up, or renovated homes.

If you have lived in your home for more than two years or you have tenant-occupied rental properties, there is an excellent chance that it cannot "compare" to recent market sold properties.

If you attempted to sell your property on the open market in "as is" condition without any fix up or clean up, you can be assured of a lower fair market price.

Based on this simple premise alone and based on what I have seen over the years, every lived-in or otherwise occupied property are valued too high based on current "as is" condition.

Because of this simple premise, most property owners should be filing tax appeals to ensure their properties are not being assessed at full retail market values. They should be assessing your property in current "as is" condition with the current defects, flaws, and wear & tear.

Unfortunately, the only way to have the TAO look at and assess your property in current "as is" condition is for you to to go through the property tax appeal process.

CHAPTER 3: FAIR MARKET VALUE

> DETERMINING FAIR MARKET VALUE

Every property assessment begins with determining the fair market value (FMV) of a property. Once FMV is established, in Georgia, 40% of that value is assessed to calculate the property tax you owe. This does not include any special assessments that may be added later.

Many property owners have a general idea what their property value is. They know the price range their property falls under and make a "guesstimation". However, most will not be able to write a specific value without some outside assistance.

For many people that outside assistance often comes from:

> Zillow or some other online real estate database

> Multiple listing system (MLS) that real estate licensees use

> Real estate appraiser

> Real estate agent or real estate broker

Unless you are in the real estate industry, it is generally difficult for a non-licensed person to access the MLS in your area. MLS are not typically marketed towards non-licensed individuals. MLS are generally marketed to real estate professionals and real estate companies.

And even if you have access to the MLS, not all MLS are created equal. MLS are traditionally not very user-friendly and can overwhelm many users due to its complexity.

Zillow is probably the most accessible and one of the easiest real estate databases online but I do not consider it an MLS in the traditional sense due to its many limitations.

The problem with Zillow is that it does not provide all the information you may need to get a good fair market value. Certainly, Zillow is better than nothing but it is not a substitute for accessing MLS data.

> WHEN TO DETERMINE FAIR MARKET VALUE

Because I generally file multiple property appeals for myself, associates, and clients every year, I am not always able to do a full valuation analysis on every property by the appeal deadline. I generally do a cursory analysis at first.

I have access to a couple of local MLS and so I can run a quick report of prior year sales for some properties. But I will not necessarily scrutinize each one in detail if I am time-crunched and coming up on a deadline.

This is why I advise people to write a lower value on the appeal form even if it seems "ridiculous" at the time. You want to cover yourself. You can find that you end up negotiating against yourself later or you find other reasons and factors that justify a lower value.

I will scan the range of sold prices of prior year properties in the neighborhood and select a lower value number to write on the appeal form. However, this number is not finalized until I am ready to print the appeal form, sign it, and deliver it.

The bottom line is: the more research you can do upfront, the better. However, if you get busy like I do, it is not the end of the world if you have to guess at the value and then round it down sufficiently to cover yourself later.

> BEFRIEND A REAL ESTATE AGENT

I generally recommend property owners contact and become acquainted with a real estate agent or real estate broker. (In Georgia, a real estate broker is a "higher" license than a real estate salespersons license.)

There are literally tens of thousands of licensed real estate agents throughout Georgia. Most active licensed agents will have access to their local MLS. Most active licensed agents are looking to establish and meet new contacts.

Depending on your persistence and how nicely you ask, there is a good chance you will find a friendly real estate agent (or broker) to help and provide you with MLS info to help determine the fair market value of your property and neighborhood.

I recommend being honest in your approach. Don't lie or mislead them to get what you want. You may find that a friendly real estate agent (or broker) to be an important contact in your future if you ever decide to buy, sell, or lease property. They may also have other valuable contacts. Be nice and don't burn a real estate agent (or broker).

If you are lucky enough to be acquainted with a real estate appraiser, they may also assist you. A local appraiser will have access to your local MLS. However, there are far fewer real estate appraisers than there are real estate agents. And they may be more sensitive to providing you free information in determining fair market value. After all, they are in the property valuation business.

Be honest, be friendly, be respectful. I am confident you will find the right person and get the information you need or want.

> WHAT YOU NEED TO DETERMINE FAIR MARKET VALUE

What you want from either a real estate agent or real estate appraiser is: 12-months of sales comparables (sales comps) for your neighborhood of the PRIOR Year.

Let me say this again because it is very important to understand. What you want is to get 12-months of sales comparables for your property of the PRIOR year.

Believe it or not, most licensed real estate agents are unfamiliar with the property tax appeal process. Most of their advice regarding property taxes is to make sure you file homestead exemption if you intend to live in it. It's very basic, low-level advice and unrelated to what I cover in this book.

Even those real estate agents that have heard of property tax appeals don't know you need PRIOR year sales comps, not current year sales comps.

Most licensed real estate agents will instinctively look up and provide sales comparables for the most recent three-to-six month period.

That is absolutely NOT what you want for property tax appeal purposes!

If you don't specify that you want 12-months worth of sales comps of the **prior year**, they will likely provide the most recent sales comps. This will hurt your efforts.

Obviously, you want to handle this delicately. Don't be disrespectful, rude, or impatient in your request. If you are provided the most recent comps, you want to gently tell them that "for the purposes of property tax appeals", you need prior year sales comps.

In theory, the TAO is supposed to assess the property based on the value effective January 1 of the current year.

For example, assessment notices issued in 2025 are supposed to based on fair market values effective January 1, 2025.

In order to determine the FMV effective January 1, 2025, an analysis has to be done from comparable sales from January 1 to December 31, 2024.

With certain properties where there are few comparable sales, you might even have to ask for 2023 sales comps. That is what some TAOs do when they deal with properties with few comparable sales. They sometimes go back further than the prior year's data.

The mass appraisal system that all TAOs use to determine values for assessment notices is highly imperfect. The mass appraisal system does not take into account specific or unusual situations of individual properties without manual inspections and manual adjustments.

Although property appraisers at TAOs sometimes proactively make adjustments to properties in certain areas, they simply cannot do a physical inspection of every property in a county. They don't have the manpower for it.

It falls upon property owners to inform and update their TAO with information that may impact the valuation of their property.

Depending on where your property is located, you may find that nearly all the sales comps of a neighborhood are of updated, fixed-up retail-ready homes. In those situations, the sales comps will skew high.

With some properties, the sales comps will show other older, worn-down property. However, even then, it is not a foregone conclusion that the average or median sales comps is actually indicative of the actual FMV of your property.

That is why, ideally, you want both the MLS sales comparables data and the MLS photos of each sales comp for that entire calendar year, if you can. You can get a fuller picture of your property's standing compared to actual sales with photos.

There is no precise formula to determining specific value. There are only methods to determine an "estimated value". You cannot simply take the average number because it doesn't take into account individual property characteristics or condition. Even using a square-footage formula is imperfect because of the need for manual adjustments.

You can have two real estate appraisers evaluate the same property and come up with two different values. Also, your opinion as a property owner may be different from any real estate professional.

Oftentimes, you will hear property owners say that if they could sell their rental property for what the TAO values them at, they would. I find that many experienced property owners have a good pulse on the general value of their properties.

As the property owner, you are the final decision maker of what value you will put down on the tax appeal form. You can put any number you want down but you should be prepared to defend it.

On a property tax appeal, if you are ever in doubt, write a lower value even if it seems ridiculous at that time.

I've made the mistake of writing down a "reasonable value" only to later regret it because I uncovered data, research, or circumstances that justified a lower value.

You don't want to negotiate against yourself or sabotage yourself in the tax appeal process. I have, unfortunately, made this mistake several times.

Again, if you are ever in doubt, write a lower value. You can always agree to a higher number later in the process but you cannot agree to a lower number than you wrote.

Tax Assessor Comparables

Getting sales comps from friendly real estate agents is not always easy. I know this from experience. Before I had personal and professional connections or had my own MLS access, I was blind when it came to sales comps. However, there is an alternative source to get your sales comps. You ask for sales comps from your TAO.

In theory, all TAOs pull and compile sales comps from MLS and other systems into their mass appraisal system.

Sales comps are supposed to establish and support values they assign to individual properties.

However, this is an imperfect system because every property is unique. No two properties are completely identical. Properties can be very similar but it is impossible for them to be identical.

TAO staff is supposed to check and scrutinize that each sales comp is suitable for any given property. However, due to the sheer volume of parcels and the overall workload they have, there are often mistakes made.

When you ask for sales comps from the TAO, you are checking to see if the ones they are using are actually appropriate. In my experience, TAO sales comps are not always appropriate or suitable.

There are various reasons why some sales comps won't be suitable. They could be in another subdivision, they could be too far, or the property itself is too dissimilar.

Sales comps you get from TAOs will not come with nice photos or helpful real estate agent comments you find with MLS sales comps. TAOs generally only provide "blind" barebone information. Be prepared for this.

You will have to take extra steps to take their list of sales comps and supplement it with additional research. For example, you may have to do Google Street View searches to see the exterior condition of a property or view the neighborhood.

Some TAO staff will be lazy and tell you to use their public online search tool to find your own sales comps. I can tell you from experience, their online systems are practically useless. It's a waste of time.

You should insist that they provide you a list of the sales comps they used for your property's assessment. It is generally a one-page or two-page report.

In theory, this is a report they use during appeal settlement negotiations and in the BOE hearings. What you are looking for is to make sure the sales comps they are using are appropriate. You should also identify those that aren't suitable and have them disqualified.

CHAPTER 4: EVALUATING YOUR PROPERTY

> HOW TO INSPECT YOUR PROPERTY

I've inspected many properties over the years and I always find defects, damage, and imperfections in any property. The reason for that is that houses are never built perfectly.

The dirty little secret that most people don't know is that even new houses and new construction are full of imperfections and defects from the very beginning. "New" does not equal "perfect" when it comes to construction of homes.

Because of this, I know that every property will have defects and deficiencies going in. It is all a matter of degree. Some of them matter, others don't matter very much.

With any property and with enough time, all properties, even unoccupied ones, experience damage, physical depreciation, and general wear-and-tear. Some of them matter, some of them don't. Again, it is all a matter of degree.

I say this because most property owners are biased. They sometimes magnify issues that are less important or they minimize issues that should be called out and notated in a tax appeal.

When evaluating your own property, it is best to inspect the "big stuff" first (most expensive and most visible items) and work your way down to less important, less expensive items.

I generally recommend people start with the exterior first because it is the most visible and what will most likely be inspected and photographed by the county appraisers.

> DEFECTS, DEFICIENCIES, & DEFERRED MAINTENANCE

Whenever I evaluate property for an appeal, I immediately seek out "the Three D's" for inspecting a property. They are: Defects, Deficiencies, and Deferred Maintenance (DDD).

It is unimportant to distinguish between a property defect vs. property deficiency vs. a deferred maintenance issue. What is important is that they are identified, notated, and photographed. You should identify both seen and unseen issues within a property that will LOWER property value.

The general question to ask yourself is: "What are the things about this property that would lower my sales price if a buyer knew about it?"

When people sell their property, they tend to emphasize the positive features & attributes and minimize the negative attributes.

When filing a property tax appeal, you do the reverse. You emphasize the negative attributes and minimize the positive attributes.

When filing a property tax appeal, this is the time to bring attention to any or all negative attributes (DDD) that would negatively affect the sales price (i.e. market value).

The general priority I recommend is to start with the most significant items first. They are the most visible and most costly parts of a property.

Depending on the age of your property, some of it will be obvious. Any damages or repair items would go on your list.

For example, you could have wood damage, siding damage, an old/declining HVAC system, an old and worn roof, or a property that badly needs new paint.

General "wear and tear" is not always an obvious item. The question you have to ask yourself is that if you emptied out the house and broom swept it, would the property be able to sell for market value?

Having been a real estate investor and property owner for many years, I can assure you that even in a broom-swept property, there are many deficiencies that can be found.

Old carpet, damaged flooring, dinged or damaged walls & hallways that need paint or repair, banged up doors & doorways, water damage in kitchen, bath, and laundry areas.

It is amazing what you can find when all contents are moved out.

I am not suggesting that you move all contents out of a property to evaluate or inspect it. What I am saying is that you should visualize all the undesirable things you would find if the property was empty.

You want to make a list of all DDD items you can find and then attribute a dollar item that would be required to cure the problem.

For larger items, it is helpful for documentation purposes to have a work estimate or repair quotes from reputable contractors to fix those items. For things you don't have a quote for, you assign dollar values to it.

When dealing with DDD items, photos are your best tools to convey the overall condition and specific items you want to show. I will get into the issue of what photos you need to take and how to take them later in this book.

> EXTERIOR INSPECTION

Those most obvious place to start inspecting and getting photos is the exterior of the house. I typically walk around the house and look at the roof, fascia, soffit, siding, paint, foundation, and anything that might detract from getting full value of the property if it were placed for sale on the open market.

Property photos taken by most real estate appraisers and many real estate agents are generally "straight on" photos with few angles.

These photos are meant to be flattering and pleasing visually. They tend to be balanced and symmetrical photos that enhance positive features and attributes. They also obscure negative attributes. These types of photos are generally not helpful to your cause.

Part of why this occurs, is because they are intentionally portraying the house in a positive light. Straight-on, "no-angle" photos of a property where a viewer stands at center facing the front or rear of a property is an unrealistic, sanitized view of the property.

The reality is that when anyone inspects a property, very few people are standing out on the center of a sidewalk directly looking at the front of the house. Very few people stand in the center of the backyard to look directly at the rear exterior of the house.

In a real-life exterior inspection, people tend to walk around the house moving their head up and down, and turning their head left and right as they are walking.

Consciously or not, there are inspecting and viewing the property with both depth and dimension.

The views they see as they walk around are angular views with depth. Angular views show much more depth than if you view a property directly straight center.

With today's smartphones and built-in cameras, you should take many photos from different angles. Don't be skimpy about it.

The idea is to take more photos than you need so that you can select and cull them later to the photos that will best tell your story.

Exterior Walls & Siding

As you inspect the exterior of your property, you may find cracks, weather-damage, or other issues with on the exterior walls and siding. You want to get photos and notate them.

However, depending on the size of the of the damage, they can be difficult to convey visually if you don't also include a window for context.

Without a window in the photograph for context, a photo with cracks or damage is too generic to tell the story.

Windows

Over time, window seals break down and you will have moisture that seeps into window panes. Or with older homes, you might see water or wood damage on the interior side of bathroom windows. Or you may have cracked windows panes with rental property.

With older property, you may find various issues with windows that is worth photographing and notating.

Fascia & Soffit

Fascias and soffits often experience weather or moisture damage over time. Paint peels and crack over time. They are good areas to get photos. They are highly visible and have an outsized influence of whether a property looks good or not.

Roofs

If you have an older roof (15-years or more), it is worth getting photos of the roof to see if there are damaged or missing shingles due to storms and wind. You also want to inspect the condition of the shingles overall.

Depending on the type of property you are dealing with and how steep the roof pitch is, you (or someone you know) may be able to climb a ladder and get on the roof to get some roof photos.

However, there are many properties which are tall and have a steep roof pitch. In those situations, it is generally unsafe for anyone besides a professional to climb on the roof.

Steep pitch roofs are sometimes easier to inspect from the ground especially if you step back from the property.

Sometimes, the only way to safely get good photos of the roof is to use a drone.

The importance of inspecting and evaluating the condition of a roof cannot be overstated. Newer roofs in great condition preserves the value of the house. Older and damaged roofs can severely reduce the market value of a property.

If you have an old or worn roof, you should make getting roof photos a priority.

HVAC

A good HVAC system preserves the value of a property. An older HVAC system (10+ years) can lower the value of a property.

The most obvious indicator of how old an HVAC system is inspecting the exterior unit. An older HVAC system will show unmistakable signs of weather-wear on the exterior unit.

There might be rust stains, dents, scratches, or faded paint. When I get photos of the external HVAC unit, I get the photo from different angles.

However, I also go out of my way to get a photo of the manufacturer label.

The manufacturer label will include important information such as the serial number, model number, and manufacture date.

Sometimes the only way to determine the manufacturer of that exterior unit is to decipher the model number. You can do this through a Google search.

This is your evidence and proof that you correctly determined the age of the unit.

Other photos I get of the HVAC unit is the interior unit. This interior unit can be in a closet, the attic, or basement of the house. Interior units generally don't show age as well as exterior units because they are protected from the elements.

Obvious signs of age in an interior unit is generally from unwiped and uncleaned dust and debris in and around the unit that have collected over the years. There may be scratches and dents on and around the unit.

As such, the best way to find out the age of the interior HVAC unit is to get a photo of the manufacturer label. This can generally be found on the interior side of the cover plate.

If you feel the urge to clean the interior unit, make sure you get photos of the uncleaned unit before you wipe and clean the dust and debris away.

> INTERIOR INSPECTION

These are the major things I recommend you look at with an interior inspection. These are often unseen because it is rare that a county appraiser will inspect and walk through your house. However, interior issues are often hidden, out of sight, but sometimes significant.

Don't be afraid to criticize your house. If you want to lower the value of your tax assessment, you must be willing to adopt a critical eye of your own property whether you live in the property or you are renting it out.

Water Heater

While water heaters don't carry the same financial weight or overall value as an HVAC system, they are an essential part of any property.

An older water heater (8+ years) means you will eventually have to pay to replace it along with some of the associated plumbing.

Water heaters are generally located in a garage, laundry room, closet, attic, or basement.

What you are looking for are obvious signs of wear and age. You might see water stains and rust on the water heater.

Most importantly, you want to get a photo of the manufacturer label so you can determine the manufacture date of the water heater.

Regardless of how a water heater might appear, if a water heater is 10-years old, I would make note of it in your tax appeal write up and get the photo of the water heater and the manufacturer label. The water heater will likely need to be replaced in the near future.

Bathrooms & Kitchens

Bathrooms and kitchens experience a lot of wear and tear. Because both areas have plumbing and running water, over time, you might see water damage.

Over the course of years, you might have experienced a burst pipe, leaky seals, worn sinks & basins, malfunctioning dishwasher, or overflowing tubs or toilets. The seals in your shower could have become worn. You might have faucets and toilets that need to be replaced.

The point being is that kitchens and bathrooms are among the highest priority rooms when determining the saleability and value of a property.

A modern and updated kitchen and bathroom with new sinks, faucets, cabinets, caulk, seal, and other fixtures will be valued higher than an outdated kitchen or bathroom that have old, worn, or damaged sinks, faucets, cabinets, caulk, fixtures, etc.

Older, outdated, worn, or damaged kitchens and bathrooms are worth bringing up in a tax appeal.

Ceilings

Ceiling damage with water stains reveal moisture intrusions. You might have a roof leak. You might have a leaky pipe. Or perhaps you had a shower, tub, or sink overflow.

If you have any ceiling damage, get a photo of the ceiling damage and write down how and why you have ceiling damage.

Flooring

If you have significant flooring damage and "wear and tear", that can lower the value of your property. The issue of flooring can be very subjective.

I find that flooring suffers a lot more with tenant-occupied properties than with owner-occupied homes.

If you have very old, worn, or damaged carpet for whatever reason, get photos and notate that.

If you have damaged, cracked, loose, extremely worn, or unseated floor tiles and or hardwood planks, I would get photos and notate it.

Interior Walls & Paint

Interior walls and paint can be tricky because there is so much of it in most houses. Wear and tear of interior walls can be very different in different parts of the house.

Regardless of actual damage, if interior walls and paint look worn from years of use or the paint scheme is grossly outdated, it is worth notating.

Paint jobs are expensive and if you had to put your house up for sale and repaint the house, it would cost real money to paint the house to retail-ready condition.

> HOW TO TAKE GOOD PHOTOS

When you take photos for an appeal, you are trying to tell a story to the TAO. That story is that you have defects, deficiencies, and deferred maintenance (DDD) in your property that lowers the market value.

While I have seen a few excellently-maintained, lived-in, occupied homes, the vast majority of lived-in, occupied homes have at least some level of defects and "wear and tear," especially those that have been "lived-in" more than two years.

And with tenant-occupied homes, the "wear and tear" factor is even higher. These are not "retail-ready" homes.

When a property is not retail-ready, this generally means you cannot get the full value of a property sale compared to a similar home that is vacant, cleaned, repaired, renovated, staged, and made retail-ready.

On the open market, this means lower market value. That lower market value is what should be shown in an assessment notice but that is often not the case.

In a property tax appeal, it is insufficient to state this, you have to show this. You show this through the photos you take.

Many real estate appraisers and real estate agents dislike photos with angular views. It goes against their occupational customs and professional training.

However, when I take photos, I am trying to tell a story. I am not taking photos to sell the house. I am taking photos to show that the current condition of the property is not up to retail-ready standards.

The story I am telling in a property tax appeal is that the value on the assessment notice is too high. In order to do this, I need to communicate both in writing and photographically.

In an ideal world, we would be able to show video but that is currently not practical. So, in the property tax appeal process, we use photos to communicate visually. How you take photos matter.

You don't have to be professional photographer to learn basic techniques of visual storytelling.

For example, if you find holes, cracks, or damages in any exterior wall or siding, it is best to take the photo from an angle so that the depth and texture of the damage can be shown. There should be sufficient lighting outside to do this.

Cloudy days are not good times to take exterior photos due to poor lighting.

Late afternoons (especially in the winter) are not good times to take exterior photos due to excessive shadows. I have been guilty of this many times.

With exterior siding and exterior walls, there can be a lot of surface area compared to damaged spots you might find.

If you take a photo of only the damaged area without incorporating a window, edge, or corner into the photo to provide context, it is generic damage that looks like it can come from anywhere. This is where taking an angular shot helps.

I will often angle the camera in such a way where I take photos of damaged shots but also include a window at the very edge to give some context to the viewer the size and location of the damaged spot.

> THE COUNTY'S RIGHT TO INSPECT YOUR PROPERTY

You should know that every TAO in Georgia will declare their right to inspect your property to corroborate its condition and characteristics. If that occurs, you can expect that exterior photos of your property will be taken.

Although every TAO in Georgia theoretically has the right to inspect both the exterior **and interior** of every property, as a practical matter, they generally don't have the manpower to do this for every property and parcel in any county.

If they do inspect, they tend focus on the exterior of the property. Going inside a residential property is often a sensitive, privacy matter to most TAOs. They generally avoid "forcing" their way into most residential properties.

In almost all situations, filing a tax appeal increases the likelihood that your property will be inspected in person.

Unless you are misrepresenting the property or you have improvements and structures without permits, there is generally little concern for site inspections. It can happen without you being at the property.

Property appraisers will not break into your house to do interior inspections. And they will generally be cautious setting foot on the property itself to do an exterior inspection.

However, it is generally fair game to get whatever photos they can from the road or street.

The larger the county, the more properties, and the more tax appeals they have to deal with, the less likely property appraisers will be able to do a detailed onsite inspection when you file a tax appeal.

But most TAOs will certainly take a few photos of your property from the street during a drive-by visit.

In smaller or rural counties where there are far fewer properties and fewer tax appeals, they are much more likely to conduct a detailed onsite inspection when you file a tax appeal.

Generally, they will provide you the courtesy of a notification to avoid confrontations and misunderstandings but it is generally not required.

Even then, onsite inspections can vary. Most often, property inspections are exterior. Sometimes they do a drive-by inspection. Other times, they will get out of their vehicle and walk around the property if it is reasonably accessible and safe to do so.

If it comes up, ask the TAO when they will conduct their inspection and what they need access to.

Again, how each TAO decides and conducts their onsite inspections can vary greatly from one county to another. The general rule of thumb is that the smaller the county, the more likely they will conduct an onsite inspection.

With any onsite inspection, a property appraiser will rarely know the property better than the property owner.

For example, they may not notice that your HVAC system is 15-years old and that your water heater is 10-years old.

They may not know about missing shingles on a weak spot in the roof. They may not see water and ceiling damage caused by a bad storm, overflowing toilet, or leaky tub from years ago.

They may not see the scrapes and scuffs on certain sections of your interior wall due to children running and playing over the years.

On the chance a property appraiser decides to do an onsite

inspection, I recommend that you try to be there to help point out damages and other issues that will negatively affect your property value.

It's been my experience that property appraisers generally inspect the property to corroborate the claims on your appeal.

However, they also inspect so they can notate in their records that they reviewed the property as they are supposed to do every few years.

CHAPTER 5: FILING YOUR TAX APPEAL

> WHAT DOES IT MEAN TO "FILE A TAX APPEAL"

The word "file" confuses some people. However, the word "file" is similar to how people "file income tax returns" each year. To "file a tax appeal" simply means you fill out the required forms, print, and submit it to the tax assessor office.

In more simpler terms, to "file a tax appeal" also means "submission of a property tax appeal".

> WHEN TO FILE YOUR TAX APPEAL

On paper, you have a 45-day deadline to file your tax appeal. However, in practice, you have around 30-35 calendar days to file your tax appeal.

Depending on where you get your mail, it can take up to a week to receive an assessment notice to arrive in the mail. You automatically lose a week there. And when you file your tax appeal, you likewise want to build in some cushion time "just in case".

When it comes to tax appeals, it has been my experience that being early doesn't really help you. It only helps the TAO because they dislike the avalanche of tax appeals being filed near the deadline date.

It doesn't help you because early-filed appeal gives signals and indicators to the TAO where problem areas might be for the later-filed appeals.

For example, there might be a subdivision or an area that the mass appraisal system gets wrong. As such, there might be a disproportionate number of tax appeals coming in for that area or subdivision.

This will signal or indicate to the TAO that they might need to investigate their data further or, better yet, make them more inclined to downward adjust the value for your property.

You are more likely to get that unintended benefit if you file later in that 45-day period than if you file earlier.

Generally, I like to file my tax appeals 7-10 days before the appeal deadline. It is late enough in the process but not cutting it so close that I have to worry about a tax appeal getting lost in the mail.

> SHOULD YOU FILE YOUR APPEAL ELECTRONICALLY?

Generally, I recommend property owners file paper-based tax appeals but I do so because I teach others to do tax appeals. It's impossible to teach how to file tax appeals electronically when only a few counties have adopted an electronic tax appeal submission system.

I don't have access to all the systems to see for myself. Most of the documented tax appeal process is still paper-based, not electronic-based.

Further, I hear that different counties have different electronic appeal submission systems which further complicate the matter. I have also been told by a couple of TAOs that there are some limitations with electronic submissions.

For these and other reasons, I generally recommend filing paper-based tax appeals because it is much more tangible and you have more control over your submissions. It is still widely accepted and still the only way to file tax appeals with many Georgia counties.

For property owners in Cobb County, you want to confirm if you can scan and email your tax appeal form and documents in. I've been able to do this a couple of times in Cobb County. It is the only Georgia county I've encountered so far that allows the emailing of your tax appeal form and documents.

Other counties, such as Fulton County, insist you use their online tax appeal system if you want to file electronically.

I've begun experimenting with filing tax appeals electronically for counties that allow it. However, I am both computer and technologically savvy. Many property owners may not be. This is why I remain cautious about recommending people to file their tax appeals electronically.

When it comes to computers and technology, a lot can still go wrong whether it be user error or technical support issues but there is a lot to like when it does work.

You can bypass a lot of the tediousness and inconveniences of paper-based tax appeals by using an electronic appeal filing system, if it's available.

> APPEAL OF ASSESSMENT FORM (PT-311-A)

In Georgia, to submit a property tax appeal, you must use Georgia Form PT-311-A, the Appeal of Assessment form.

Property owners should visit their county's TAO website and download a copy of the PT-311-A there.

If you have properties in different Georgia counties, you should visit each county's TAO website separately, and download their version of the PT-311-A.

"Vanilla" vs. "Variant" forms

Unfortunately, there are many versions of PT-311-A form which can cause some confusion. Some counties customize the PT-311-A form by simply adding their agency and contact information to the "vanilla" version. Some examples of counties that do this include: Cobb, Floyd, and Muscogee counties.

Clear Form | Print Form

PT 311 A (Rev May 2020)

Cobb County Board of Tax Assessors

736 Whitlock Ave. Suite 200
Marietta, GA 30064

www.cobbassessor.org
Phone: (770) 528-3100

APPEAL OF ASSESSMENT FOR DIGEST YEAR: 2023

Appeal No: ________

Name		**Home Phone**	
Mailing		**Work Phone**	
Address			
City	**State** / **Zip**	**Email Address**	

Property / Appeal Type (Check One)

☐ Real ☐ Personal ☐ Motor Vehicle ☐ Manufactured Home

Property ID Number		**Account Number**	
Property Description	Enter Property Street Address:		

Specify Grounds for Appeal: Check all that apply	Y	N
Value	☐	☐
Uniformity	☐	☐
Taxability	☐	☐
Exemption Denial	☐	☐
Breach of Covenant	☐	☐
Denial of Covenant	☐	☐

You must select only one of the following options:

☐ BOE: appeal to the county board of equalization with appeal to superior court (any/all grounds)

* ☐ ARBITRATION: to arbitration with appeal to superior court (valuation is only grounds that may be appealed to arbitration)

* ☐ HEARING OFFICER: for (1) non-homesteaded real property (and contiguous real property) or (2) wireless personal property account(s) with an aggregate FMV in excess of $500,000, to a hearing officer with appeal to superior court (value and uniformity only)

* ☐ SC: Directly to Superior Court (requires consent of BOA) (any / all grounds)

* Additional Cost / Fees May Apply

Owner's Value Assertion (Required) $ ________

Property Owner Comments

Property Class ☐ Residential ☐ Commercial ☐ Industrial ☐ Agricultural ☐ Other: ____________

Signature of Property Owner or Agent **Date**

NOTE: If the appeal form is signed by an agent, a letter of authorization must accompany the filing of the appeal.

Agent's Address: ________________ **Agent's Phone #** ________

Agent's Email Address ________

NOTE: Filing of this document will create a review of the County's assessment. Reasonable notice is herein provided that an onsite inspection of the subject property by a member of the county appraisal staff may be performed.

Assessors Use Only		**Previous Year Value**	**Taxpayer's Returned Value**	**Current Year Value**
	100%			
	40%			

Date Received: **Received By:**

It is not a catastrophic situation if you use a "vanilla" version of the appeal form.

In theory, every county should accept the "standard" appeal form found on the Georgia Department of Revenue website.

But I prefer to adhere to local TAO customs whenever possible.

In any case, the intake clerks at your TAO are trained to review incoming appeal forms. They will contact or inform you if you have used an incorrect appeal form.

Some Georgia counties use other versions of the PT-311-A form which I consider "variant" forms. These counties use reformatted or redesigned "variant" forms that are dramatically different from the "vanilla" PT-311-A form.

You should pay special attention to download the county-specific version of the PT-311-A form. Some examples of counties that use "variant" appeal forms include: Fulton, DeKalb, and Chatham.

In smaller and more rural counties of Georgia, you will likely see them use the "vanilla" PT-311-A form.

Please note that the official "vanilla" version of the PT-311-A form can be found on the Georgia Department of Revenue website.

Downloading your county's correct PT-311-A form is the first crucial step to filing your tax appeal.

Because there are variants of the PT-311-A form, going forward, I will be referencing the "vanilla" PT-311-A appeal form. You will have to make minor adjustments for the "variant" appeal forms.

Notice: Government websites frequently add, change, and modify the content of their websites. As such, web hyper-links frequently change. The best way to find the aforementioned appeal forms for your county is through a Google or Bing search.

> FILLING OUT THE PT-311-A FORM

Contact Information

When you fill out the PT-311-A form, be careful to clearly write all your contact information. That includes your preferred mailing address, phone number, and email address.

Do not put the street address of the property being appealed unless you actually live there or receive U.S. postal mail there!

If you do not write or fill-in the correct mailing address, you may not receive any mailed notices. It is important you receive all written letters and notices regarding your tax appeal.

Do not write phone numbers or email addresses you do not regularly check!

I know some people don't regularly check email. They are tech-averse. However, the TAO occasionally calls and email property owners for additional information. They also use it to follow up on other matters relating to your appeal.

If you don't respond timely to TAO emails, you might give them the false impression you ignored them or simply don't care about your appeal.

Property / Appeal Type

Within this book, I assume you are filing a tax appeal on your home or rental property. You will check the box "Real" or "Real Property" depending on the version of the PT-311-A form you are using.

Property ID Number

This field is very important to get right. This is the unique identifier for your property. Many cities have properties which have very similar street addresses. This can create unnecessary confusion.

For example, compare 2200 6th *Ave.* vs. 2200 6th *St.* vs. 2200 6th *Dr.*

Do you see how this can potentially be a mess without a unique property identifier number?

The unique property identifier number ensures that everyone is discussing the correct property regardless of street address.

This unique number is listed on the Property ID number from the PT-306 Annual Assessment Notice. You want to carefully write that number on the appeal form.

Property Description

In this field, I typically write the property street address as most ordinary people would reference a property.

Please note that I intentionally disregard the Property Description field from the PT-306, Annual Assessment Notice, as a matter of personal preference.

I do so because I think the property street address is more helpful in this situation. No one is going to know what property is being appealed simply by reading the Property ID number.

However, with the property street address listed in this field, it makes it easier for everyone to know at a glance. Having filed 250+ tax appeals in Georgia, no one has ever complained about how I fill in the Property Description.

Account Number

The account number can be found on the PT-306 Annual Assessment Notice. I don't view this as an important field but I will fill it in if I have it.

Specify Grounds for Appeal

For the purpose of this book, most tax appeals are for single-family homes or rental homes. Most property owners will check the "Value" box because that is what is being contested most times.

The "Value" box means that you are appealing the fair market value and subsequently the assessed value. The "Uniformity" box is if you believe that your property is not being assessed consistently or similarly to another equivalent property.

You might consider checking the "Uniformity" box if you feel you need to. But recently, I've gotten mixed feedback whether it's advantageous to check the "Uniformity" box at all. I used to recommend people check the "Uniformity" box but I've gone back to checking only the "Value" box for now. One day, I hope to get a clear or better answer when it's advantageous to check the "Uniformity" box or not.

Appeal Hearing Options

For people with single-family homes and rental properties less than $500,000, you will check off the "Board of Equalization" box.

This is the easiest, least expensive, and most common hearing method to appeal property for homeowners and landlords. The BOE option is what we discuss and cover in this book.

Owner's Value Assertion

This field is required and very important. I have an entire section in this book devoted to how to determine fair market value (FMV) for your property.

In general, if you are uncertain as to the fair market value, it is better to put a lower value than higher value. You can always agree to a higher value later but you will not be able to negotiate below the value you write if you get it wrong.

85% vs. 100% Billing

In some counties, you will be asked to choose 85% or 100% billing. During a property tax appeal, counties will require at least 85% payment of estimated property taxes due.

The idea is that if you file a tax appeal, there is a fair chance you will reduce the property taxes due after the tax appeal process is completed. As such, property owners who pay 100% of the estimated taxes will likely overpay.

Property owners who prefer not to "overpay" can choose the 85% option. However, there is still a fair chance property owners will still receive a second property tax bill after the tax appeal process is over.

The downside of choosing the 85% option is that some mortgage companies will only pay the first property tax bill, not the follow-up bill. That means the property owner will have to come out of pocket for the follow-up tax bill.

One particular year, there were a few properties that had follow-up bills after the tax appeal process was over. I thought the mortgage company would automatically cover the follow-up bills. But I ended up incurring late penalties and interest charges when I found out the mortgage company did not pay the follow-up bill. It annoyed me tremendously and was a tough lesson.

This is why I recommend that people who have mortgages to choose the 100% billing option. If your property tax bill is lower after the tax appeal process is over, you should receive a tax refund payment back to your mortgage escrow account or a check will be mailed to you.

Ultimately, it is a matter of personal preference and how you handle personal and business finance matters.

Property Owner Comments

There is never enough space to write complete comments. Because of this, I always include an attachment with additional and expanded comments with photos.

Because I know that every appeal I file will include additional attachments with additional information, I only use the Property Owner Comments section to highlight the most important points.

There is not much space to write in this section. You write only the highlights, nothing more.

I don't write complete sentences here. I list several bullet points and short phrases, from the most significant to the least significant. I make sure to make reference to a separate attachment and photos so they know there is more detail and substance to your appeal.

For example, I might write: old HVAC system, old water heater, high crime area, missing shingles on roof, water damage in bathroom, worn carpet, sales comps $100-$150K range, etc. See attached statement and photos.

Property Class

In this book, we focus only single-family homes. As such, you should check the "Residential" box. This box is also appropriate for duplexes and triplexes.

However, in Georgia, if your property has 4-units or more, you would check the "Commercial" box.

Agent Section

When you file a property tax appeal, you have the option to designate an "agent" to represent your interests in the appeal.

If you wish to designate an agent, write-in their name and contact information which includes their mailing address, phone number, and email address.

"Agent" Explained

In the context of a property tax appeal, an "agent" is anyone you designate to represent you or help represent you in the appeal. This is not to be confused with "real estate agent", "insurance agent", or any other occupational or professional titles you might think of.

An "agent" can be a friend, family member, business associate, or hired professional. Who you designate as an agent depends on what you expect or want the agent to do.

An agent named on your appeal can:

> Receive phone calls and written notices on your behalf

> Inquire information regarding the property and the tax ap-

peal

> Make phone calls and submit written communications on your behalf

> Appear virtually or in-person at appeal hearings

> Perform specific tasks relating to the tax appeal

For example, you can designate a friend or family member as your agent to be a backup person to receive written notices on your behalf.

In some Georgia counties, both the property owner and agent receives copies of all written notices and notifications. **However, you should always ask to confirm and be safe.**

For example, I recently learned the hard way that the TAO in Dekalb county only sends written notices to the agent, not the property owner. This was inconvenient because I wrongly assumed that the property owner would also get their notices.

Another example, you can designate a paid professional to do all the work and fully represent you on all aspects of the appeal.

It all depends on you and the scope of support you want from your agent.

For example, I have had property owners designate me as their agent on their property tax appeals to fully represent them.

In other instances, I allow some property owners I know to list me as their agent so I can be their backup person and be their second pair of eyes to all written letters and notices.

The property owner assumes primary responsibility for their own tax appeals but I am listed as agent for the purpose of backing them up.

Please note that you do not have to designate an agent upfront on the appeal form if you are unsure. You can always designate an agent later through a written Letter of Authorization (LOA) to the tax assessors office. But I find it easier and more efficient to designate the agent upfront, if at all possible.

Caution When Designating Agents

In theory, when you are the property owner, you should be able to write the agent's name, mailing address, phone number, and then SIGN on the signature line in the Agent section.

In theory, that should be sufficient designate your agent on your tax appeal.

Unfortunately, people have reported getting friction from a few TAOs for strictly following the written requirements on the PT-311-A form:

> *NOTE: If the appeal form is signed by an agent, a letter of authorization must accompany the filing of the appeal.*

In other words, if the property owner writes in the agent's name, contact information, and signs it, it **should** be enough to designate an agent on the appeal form.

However, what happens is that when the appeal form is submitted, the clerk that receives incoming tax appeal forms REFUSES to accept the appeal form unless there is an attached written Letter of Authorization!

The clerk misunderstands that an attached Letter of Authorization (LOA) is **not** required when the property owner signs the appeal form.

A LOA is technically only required when the agent fills in and submits the appeal form with the agent's signature.

This is an important distinction!

I've been able to overcome this occasional misunderstanding by escalating the matter to a more knowledgeable worker but it is a hassle.

I had one property owner tell me he was forced to scribble a note on the spot to attach to his prepared appeal form when the clerk declined to accept his completed appeal form.

I had another property owner tell me that another clerk gave her friction for not including a LOA although she was the property owner signing the appeal form.

Based on these incidents, I now recommend as a precautionary measure that anyone who wishes to designate an agent on the appeal form to also attach an originally-signed LOA regardless of who is submitting or signing the appeal.

A LOA can be short and simple but you must have an original-signature preferably with a blue-ink pen.

Sample Letter of Authorization (LOA) for Agent

I believe in keeping things simple. Here is sample wording for a very basic authorization letter.

I am the property owner of 123 ABC Street, Property ID: 123456789.
I hereby appoint John Doe as my agent for my tax appeal.

Sincerely,
Property Owner Name

I provide this example not to be followed literally but to show that you that basic writing skills is all that is needed for a basic LOA. So, don't overthink this.

Sign the Appeal Form

I hate that I have to write and explain the following because it seems so petty but this has been an annoying area of friction I have encountered.

When you sign the appeal form, PT-311-A or letters of authorization, I highly recommend you sign with a blue-ink pen.

The reason why is that some TAOs closely scrutinize signatures on appeal forms more than others.

Years ago, I had a couple of TAO employees ask me to my face if I signed the form or used a digital signature. They even held my appeal forms up to the light to scrutinize my signature. I told them the truth. I signed the form myself with a black-ink pen.

Because of these annoying and insulting incidents, I now tell everyone to signing with a blue-ink pen. Sign with a blue-ink pen so that there is no question the signature on the appeal form is an original signature.

> DELIVER YOUR TAX APPEAL

When you complete filling out the PT-311-A appeal form and sign it with an original signature, you have to deliver it to your TAO. You can either hand-deliver your appeal or mail it in.

If you can, it is always best to drive it in and hand-deliver your appeal in person. If you hand-deliver it, they will generally review your appeal form and attachments on the spot to catch any obvious errors.

If you designate an agent on your appeal form, this is when you might get some friction if you didn't attach a LOA.

They will generally time-stamp the appeal form on the spot. They should provide you a photocopy of the time-stamped appeal form before you leave.

I remind everyone that there are 159 counties in Georgia and each county will have their own way of processing hand-delivered appeal forms. Be prepared for the unexpected and be flexible.

Whenever you visit a TAO, you generally have the option to meet with a property appraiser or TAO employee to ask further questions you might have regarding the appeal process. It is also good to put faces to names whenever you can.

There are intangible benefits to going in person, meeting the staff, and getting a personal feel for things.

Having said all that, it is not always practical to hand-deliver appeals because of the drive-time and distance to reach a TAO.

For example, Fulton County is a huge county in the metro Atlanta area. Driving from north Fulton to the Fulton County TAO in downtown Atlanta can take nearly an hour each way depending on traffic.

While it is certainly possible to drive the appeal in, most metro Atlanta residents in outlying areas don't have the tolerance or patience to drive into downtown Atlanta to hand-deliver an appeal. The hassle and time involved is too much and I can't blame them.

Sometimes, it is just easier to pay the postage to mail it in.

Depending on how many pages you are including with your appeal form, I generally recommend using a large envelope that will comfortably hold several pages of 8.5" x 11" paper.

You minimize the chance of damaging the enclosed documents by mailing it flat vs. trying to fold and crease your documents and squeezing it into a smaller envelope.

When a TAO clerk receives your original appeal form and submissions, they will generally scan your documents into their computer system. There is a much better chance of minimizing damages to your original documents if clerks don't have to contend with inconvenient folds and creases in the paper.

So, mail your appeal forms in flat, not folded or creased.

Risks of Mailing In Your Appeal

If you choose to mail it in, you have to be prepared for the small possibility that your appeal could get lost in the mail or be unexpectedly delayed.

As a general rule, as long as you postmark your envelope before the deadline date, it shouldn't matter when the TAO physically receives your appeal. They are supposed to honor the postmark.

Let me say that I've been fortunate. I've never had any appeals I've been involved with get lost in the mail. But I am not oblivious to the fact that it could happen one day, however remote a chance that might be.

Your chances of protecting yourself against non-delivery or

mis-delivery of your appeal submission is much better if you use U.S. Priority Mail or Certified Mail to mail in your appeal. You can also use UPS or Fedex, if necessary.

I frequently use inexpensive First-Class Mail to deliver appeals to the TAO knowing that I would follow-up on with a phone call or email.

Even if my original appeal submission got lost, I was prepared to either hand-deliver before the deadline or mail another original copy postmarked before the deadline.

Of course, this backup system only works if you mail it in at least one week prior to the deadline and if you are within driving distance of your TAO.

If you are up against the deadline or the TAO is too far to hand-deliver, you absolutely should consider using U.S. Priority Mail, Certified Mail, or other tracked delivery method.

Of course, keep a copy of your receipt and tax appeal submission.

Special Note for Cobb County Property Owners

If you are filing a tax appeal in Cobb County, they may allow you to email your tax appeal form and documents in. I've done this a few times and it's very convenient.

If you do this, make sure you request email confirmation that they received your tax appeal documents.

CHAPTER 6: AFTER YOUR SUBMIT YOUR APPEAL

> WAITING PERIOD

After you deliver your tax appeal, there is generally a long period of waiting for an official response to your appeal.

Until recently, I've told people they can expect to wait at least 90-days for a response. However, in late 2022, I noticed that nearly every county I was tracking was running long in getting a response.

I've been told that TAOs are allowed 180-days (6-months) to respond to your tax appeal. As it stands now, I don't recommend you wait that long without follow-up.

After 90-days, I recommend that you follow-up at least once a month to find out if a mailed response has been sent to you.

You will either receive a "NO CHANGE" Letter or you will receive a revised Notice of Assessment (PT-306C).

> "NO CHANGE" LETTER

A "NO CHANGE" letter "officially" means that the TAO reviewed your appeal and they believe their original assessment is correct.

Your appeal case will automatically be forwarded to the BOE for scheduling.

I have learned from personal experience and keeping my ears to the ground that a "NO CHANGE" letter can mean several things beyond the official meaning.

Unofficial Reasons for "No Change" Letter

I want to emphasize that I am sharing my *opinion* based on personal experience and informal conversations. This is in no way considered "official" information or advice.

Unfortunately, there is a lot that goes on within a TAO than most property owners realize. This is why I say, you may not want to know how the sausage is made.

The property appraiser working your appeal occasionally runs out of time to do in-depth research into your property and tax appeal.

It is easier to kick the can down the road and respond with a "NO CHANGE" letter to meet their internal deadline.

Your appeal and information might be valid but not overwhelmingly so. The TAO takes the unstated position if the property owner feels strong enough, they can continue the appeal.

TAOs engage in the game of attrition. Only the most persistent property owners will push forward. In other words, they kick the can down the road if they can.

I was told directly more than once by an informed source that some TAOs don't want to be put in the position of lowering assessed values.

If the values need to be lowered, they prefer to point the fingers to the BOE for lowered values.

It keeps the TAO from being criticized for lowering assessed values too much thus hurting overall property tax collections. It is a CYA move decided by some TAO leaders to protect their own jobs.

Quite frankly, there is political pressure to keep assessed values higher in order to increase the tax collections.

I generally try to avoid any references to politics but in this case when someone from inside tells me to my face, it is hard to deny political pressure influences how TAO's operate and process appeals.

The bottom line is, regardless of underlying reason, your appeal case is moved to the BOE.

> REVISED NOTICE OF ASSESSMENT (PT-306C)

Occasionally, a TAO will issue a revised notice of assessment (PT-306C) with a lowered assessed value.

A PT-306C (C=Change) looks very similar to original notice of assessment (PT-306). That is intentional. The revised assessment notice is meant to be a replacement assessment notice for a property owner to consider.

The biggest difference between the PT-306C and PT-306 is the text box in the upper right-hand corner of the form.

Instead of a 45-day deadline to submit an appeal, you are provided a 30-day deadline to submit a written continuation.

Remember, the 30-day deadline is calculated from when the TAO issued the PT-306C, not when you actually received it.

Fortunately, the PT-306C shows the deadline date so you don't have to calculate it. In practical terms, by the time you receive a PT-306C, you roughly have 3-weeks to continue the appeal.

When the PT-306C is issued by a TAO, it is an opportunity for the property owner to accept the revised value and drop the appeal. Nothing has to be done to accept the value on the PT-306C.

Unfortunately, most inexperienced property owners don't understand that even if they agree with the value that the TAO presents, they will not get their property tax freeze. The assessed value will not be "frozen". The value will only be effective for that tax season.

Come the following year, they could find themselves with an escalated assessed value in which they need file a tax appeal again.

I remind Georgia property owners that there are at least **two** benefits to filing a tax appeal.

You can get the assessed value lowered for that appeal year and have that value "frozen" for another two tax years.

Even if you don't get your values lowered, the assessed value will be frozen for another two tax years only if you "go all the way" and complete the tax appeal process.

If you accept the PT-306C and don't follow through by continuing the appeal within 30-days, you will forfeit your right to freeze that value.

So, it is good news to receive a PT-306C but that is only a partial win. The bigger win comes later when you complete the tax appeal process and get that value "frozen" for the next two tax years.

To get that bigger win, you must file a continuation letter within 30-days of the print date of the PT-306C.

Bottom line? ALWAYS "continue" your appeals to get your "tax freeze".

> "CONTINUE" YOUR APPEAL

When the TAO presents you with a revised notice of Assessment PT-306C, you have 30-days to file a continuation.

It is 30-days from when the TAO issued the PT-306C, not 30-days from when you received it.

Fortunately, the PT-306C shows the deadline date so you don't have to calculate it.

A continuation letter doesn't have to be long and fancy. It can actually be quite short. The important thing is that the language is clear and that there is an original signature on the continuation letter.

Sample Continuation Letter

I have provided a simple letter template with simple wording for a basic one-page continuation letter. If you have multiple properties that you want to continue to appeal, simply add additional property entries into the body of this sample letter.

I hereby make the following request. I submit this written request for continuation of the appeal for the following property:

123 ABC Street (#012 345 678)

Thank you for your attention in this matter.

Sincerely,
Property Owner Name

Deliver Your Continuation Letter

Similar to delivering an appeal form, the continuation letter must be successfully delivered to the TAO before the deadline date if you want to preserve your appeal rights. *You want to further contest the value and then freeze that value for another two tax years.*

With the PT-311-A appeal form, I recommend that you don't deliver it too soon. However, in the case of a continuation letter, I recommend people deliver it as soon as reasonably possible.

There are no benefits to intentionally delay delivering your continuation letter.

Make sure you sign the continuation letter with an original signature using blue-ink pen.

Because you are only sending a one-page letter, it is perfectly acceptable and fine to fold the letter in thirds. Place the letter into a business-size envelope, put a first-class postage stamp on it, and then mail it.

If you don't delay mailing in your continuation letter, you will have ample time to contact the TAO to confirm they received the letter.

In the unlikely event your continuation letter is lost or mis-delivered, you still have ample time to send another one in.

Alternatively, if you are very risk-averse, there is nothing to stop you from sending one original-signed copy of your continuation letter one day and then send another original-signed copy two days later.

The chances of BOTH copies of being lost in the mail is very slim. Your cost is only two business envelopes and two first-class postage stamps.

The point of this suggestion is to help you save money and avoid the cost of unnecessarily paying U.S. Priority Mail or Certified Mail postage for a simple one-page letter.

> AFTER YOU DELIVER YOUR CONTINUATION LETTER

After you mail in your continuation letter to the TAO, there will be another period of extended waiting.

Depending on your county, you can sometimes see that status online that shows that they received your continuation letter.

The TAO will process your continuation letter and forward your appeal to the BOE for scheduling. From what I have been told, each TAO has the power to selectively forward appeals in the order they prefer.

I've been told that most BOEs will batch-forward tax appeals based on an agent's group of appeals so that they can be scheduled together.

They will often do the same thing for a property owner's group of properties so that they can be scheduled together.

Wait times can vary greatly from county to county. I find that larger counties, such as those in the metro Atlanta area, have much longer wait times than smaller counties.

CHAPTER 7: THE BOARD OF EQUALIZATION (BOE)

> WHAT IS THE BOARD OF EQUALIZATION?

The Board of Equalization (BOE) is a department that works under the county's Superior Court.

The BOE is in charge of the administration and scheduling of property tax appeal hearings called BOE hearings.

Their responsibilities include the logistics and administration of setting up meeting locations for in-person or virtual BOE hearings, mailing out notification letters, issue BOE ruling notices, and responding to customer service questions relating to BOE hearings.

BOE hearings are conducted by 3-member volunteer citizen panels who hear and rule on property tax appeal cases. I refer to them in this book as BOE member judges. They are trained by the Georgia Department of Revenue on how to conduct BOE Hearings. They have the power to approve and lower property tax assessments.

Unlike TAOs, most BOE departments are small and minimally staffed. Even in the largest counties, there is a small number of BOE staff.

Some BOE staff allow some flexibility in scheduling requests and preferences. Most do not. But it never hurts to make a request if there is a date or time you prefer.

> BOE HEARING LETTER

Whether you received a NO CHANGE letter or you submitted a continuation letter, both options lead to the BOE for scheduling.

There will be another period of extended waiting. You may not hear anything for many weeks or even months, then suddenly you will receive a BOE hearing notification letter.

BOE hearing notification letters are generally sent out 20 to 30 days prior to the hearing date. But one county, in particular, gives only two week notice for a BOE hearing. I dislike this a lot and have complained about it.

To find out more information about your county's BOE, you will need to visit your county's Superior Court website. The easiest way to find your county's BOE website is through a Google search. Unlike TAO websites, BOE websites are generally harder to find especially in smaller counties.

When you receive your BOE hearing letter, it will have several pieces of important information.

It will include:

> Time & Date of Hearing
> Street Address
> Office Location of Hearing

> BOE phone number
> BOE email address
> BOE hearing time limit (optional)

There will also be information and instructions if you wish to reschedule or cancel the BOE Hearing.

Last thing, NEVER cancel your BOE hearing even if you don't think you will or can attend. There is zero benefit to canceling the BOE hearing because if you cancel it, you also close out the possibility of utilizing a settlement conference which is an optional step after the BOE hearing.

Although I cover BOE hearings in this book, you may not have to attend one. Later in this book, I will cover how to settle your appeal case before your BOE hearing so you may not have to attend.

> BOE HEARING DATES

The scheduling of BOE Hearing dates is unpredictable and varies greatly from county to county. They are handled by the BOE department of your local Superior Court. In very small counties, it is the Superior Court clerk that will handle BOE hearings.

I have seen cases where BOE hearings are scheduled "quickly" (before December). I have seen cases where BOE hearings are scheduled well into the next calendar year.

It can be an administrative nightmare when BOE hearings from previous year tax appeals overlap with a new tax appeal season. It doesn't happen often but it does happen when a particular tax year is overloaded with an escalated number of tax appeals.

Generally, you are allowed one opportunity to reschedule. However, keep in mind, that the TAO is also allowed one reschedule request.

If you are reasonably able, keep the scheduled BOE hearing. Try not to reschedule unless you really have a good reason.

Keep in mind, BOE hearing dates are placeholder dates in case you want to attend.

I generally recommend to most property owners that they try to settle their appeal with the TAO so that they don't have to attend the BOE hearing.

I would wait to see if you can settle an appeal before exercising your right to reschedule. Every BOE office is different, but you can generally wait a few business days prior to the scheduled date to reschedule.

Generally, the later you reschedule, the later the subsequent reschedule date will be.

In my experience, BOE hearings are divided into morning and afternoon sessions. Morning sessions tend to start at 9:00 am and afternoon sessions tend to start at 1:00 pm. Again, you should check with your county's BOE for specifics.

However, *when* you actually get in front of the BOE panel can vary. It can be much later than the the scheduled start time. Generally, it is first-arrive, first-heard.

I recommend you arrive 30-minutes earlier than the scheduled time if you want to get-in and get-out sooner.

However, if you expect to run late, some BOE administrators will allow your hearing as long as you arrive prior to the conclusion of the session.

SPECIAL NOTE on Virtual BOE Hearings

Fulton and Cobb County are among the few Georgia counties that I know of that allow remote virtual BOE hearings via the ZOOM video-conferencing platform.

Virtual BOE hearings in Fulton County were born out of the 2020 COVID-19 lockdowns and is still being utilized as of the publication of this book. I have an unconfirmed report of another county utilizing virtual BOE hearings.

Virtual BOE hearings are a convenient but non-standard option for property owners. It allows you to remotely attend BOE hearings without the hassle of driving into a downtown office to attend.

You have to ask or opt-in to have a virtual BOE hearing. If you do not ask or opt-in for virtual BOE hearings in advance, you will be scheduled into a traditional in-person BOE hearing.

> PREPARE FOR YOUR BOE HEARING

The best thing you can do to prepare for your BOE hearing is to make sure you have a file folder that contains a copy of every notice and letter that the TAO and BOE have sent you in case you need to refer to them.

Have a copy of your writeup, notes, letters, repair estimates, job quotes, and printed photos in case you need to refer to them.

Don't rely on your memory. You will likely forget something in the heat of the hearing.

The next thing you can do to prepare for your BOE hearing is to request, in advance, the evidence that the TAO intends to use to support their value assessment of your property.

In larger counties, you will be limited to 15-minute BOE hearings! In other counties, there may not be any formal time limit for a BOE hearing. Find out in advance.

For residential property, they will typically provide basic photos and the sales comps they used to determine your property's assessed value.

To make this request for evidence, you must contact the BOE office or the TAO at least 10 days in advance of your hearing. Be prepared to scrutinize them closely. Sometimes inappropriate or unsuitable sales comps appear on the report and you may have to challenge them.

This also has the benefit of showing the TAO that you are taking your appeal seriously and sets the right tone for a possible appeal settlement later on.

If you really want to be prepared for your BOE hearing, you can also ask the BOE staff if you can sit in on other people's BOE hearings to see and get a feel of how a BOE hearing operates.

Technically, BOE hearings are public meetings citizens can attend but most citizens never do unless it is their own appeal hearing.

Ask to sit in on other people's BOE hearings a few days prior to your own hearing. Or you can allow other property owners to skip and go ahead of you the same day. Then, you can sit and watch their BOE hearing prior to your own BOE hearing.

I have, on occasion, sat-in on other people's BOE hearings to quietly observe and learn. It is often interesting, informative, and enlightening.

The feel and tone of BOE hearings can vary greatly. Property owners and their agents also approach their BOE hearings very differently. There is a great deal of flexibility during a BOE hearing.

When in doubt, ask for what you want and how you prefer to present your case. The worst they can do is decline your request.

Sometimes, you will have the option to choose whether you or the TAO want to present first. I always recommend allowing the TAO to present first.

Ask questions. Ask for clarification. Ask for better explanations if you need them. Don't be afraid to challenge their sales comps and assumptions if they don't make sense to you.

They don't always get it right. And they can be swayed by your reasoning, rationale, arguments, and even the passion you demonstrate.

> WHAT HAPPENS IN A BOE HEARING

In larger Georgia counties, there is a time limit for BOE hearings. The reason for that is that larger counties have many more BOE hearings to conduct than smaller counties. The time limit for a BOE hearing for large counties can be as short as 15 minutes! Each county will inform you of their time limitations, if any.

At every hearing, the BOE panel typically introduce themselves. They will explain the rules in the hearing and how the hearing will transpire.

Sometimes they will ask the property owners (or their agent) whether they want to present first. Other times, they will instruct either the TAO or property owner to present first. I recommend that you allow the TAO representative to go first, if possible.

I want to say I've been fortunate I've not had to attend many BOE hearings. For me, I attend BOE hearings only when I am required to or when I feel I cannot agree to the proposed settlement.

My anecdotal experience is that BOE hearings can vary greatly depending on who the panelists are. Some panelists are more easy-going. Other panelists prefer to run it more formally.

Either way, you should be prepared with your evidence and argument. Generally, you are asked to make four copies of your evidence. One copy for each panelist and one for yourself.

I recommend you provide an overview statement of why you are appealing, why you feel the TAO value is incorrect, and why your value is correct. I recommend you highlight and emphasize the most significant, impactful items first (items which have larger impact on value) and then work your way to the smaller items.

If applicable, you should tell them the history of the property & neighborhood, and your role with the property.

I was once accused of not being "passionate" or forceful enough in my presentation because I took a more collaborative, conversational approach and tone to my presentation.

My general personality in resolving disagreements is to collaborate and work with opposing parties and come to agreement vs. taking a forceful, adversarial approach.

I've heard stories of property owners being overly-aggressive, overly-adversarial, and overly-confrontational during their BOE hearings.

However, I do think the reverse is also true. Some property owners sell themselves short, are too passive, and defer way too much.

It's been my experience that most TAO employees don't take an adversarial or aggressive approach. They simply present their data and photos with a few comments and remarks.

However, that doesn't mean you won't encounter the rare TAO employee that will be more aggressive in their comments and presentation.

My best advice is be prepared to adjust your approach as you "read the room".

As property owners and TAO employees make their presentation, they may be peppered with a few questions by the BOE panelists along the way. Always remember, you can always asks your questions as well.

Even after all presentations are completed, they may ask a few more questions to each side.

After all presentations are completed and all questions are answered, the BOE panelists quietly confer for a few minutes and render their decision on the spot.

Be aware that decisions can sometimes be delayed with more complicated properties, valuations, and appeals.

After the hearing is over, the BOE clerk will either provide you a copy of the BOE decision before you leave or they may inform you that they will mail it to you later.

CHAPTER 8: SETTLE YOUR TAX APPEAL

> HOW TO SETTLE YOUR APPEAL

The most efficient way of resolving your tax appeal and getting your tax freeze is to settle your appeal with the TAO.

Specifically, you want to contact the TAO appraiser who is working on your appeal and see if they are open to discussing and settling the appeal without either of you having to attend a BOE hearing.

Sometimes the property appraiser working your appeal will contact you to see if you are interested in discussing and settling the appeal.

That is generally the best-case scenario because it shows interest and motivation on their end to resolve cases without having to go through the BOE.

This is a win-win situation if you and the county appraiser are willing to be flexible, compromise, and can find common ground.

In order to successfully do this, it is important that you demonstrate you know your property, its flaws, imperfections, damage, and deferred maintenance issues better than they do. The easiest way to do this is to direct them to photos you should have provided earlier.

You should also know the fair market value of your property that is supported by prior year sales comps in hand. You should explain any manual adjustments you make and justify them.

If you did not provide photos earlier, now is the time to email them photos that shows that the flaws, imperfections, damage, and deferred maintenance which lowers the market value of your property.

It is important that you set the right tone. The "right tone" can vary from one appraiser to another. Generally, you want to be professional and firm in your convictions.

You want them to understand you will do what you need to do to win your appeal even if that means showing up in person to the BOE hearing.

If they believe you are committed to show up at a BOE hearing, they may be more inclined to settle with you now while they are in control than later at a BOE hearing.

I've found that every person's level of conviction is different in these situations. Some people have conviction but do not know how to represent themselves, explain their property, its condition, and other factors they believe lowers the property value.

Some people say they have conviction until it becomes too stressful or inconvenient. Other people who are experienced won't bluff. They carry out what they say they will do.

The more prepared you are, the more conviction you have, the more ability you have to follow through, the better your chances are in negotiating a settlement.

Settlement negotiations with a TAO appraiser doesn't have to be long or stressful. TAO appraisers know they are dealing with private citizens in these matters.

They will usually not try to overwhelm you with technical jargon. They have an idea of what values they will settle on and what they will not.

They will often rely on the sales comps they have on record. But you can lean into information they do not have or they cannot see for themselves. This is why photos are very important in any property tax appeal case. You also have the right to challenge their sales comps if you feel they are not representative or suitable.

The better informed you are and the more prepared you are, the more likely they will soften their position and be persuaded towards your direction.

It can be tricky to figure it out. Sometimes you have to ask directly, "What is the best value you think you can offer to settle this?"

You always have the right to pause your settlement discussion to think about it and revisit later.

In a sense, you want to sell them on the idea of settling with you. Because if they do not settle with you, they will have to go through the hassle of formally preparing their case, prepare a presentation, show up at the BOE hearing, and then present it at the BOE hearing.

Most TAO appraisers carry a huge caseload every year. Often, they are stretched thin. TAO appraisers are generally not high-paying positions. There is frequent turnover in most TAOs.

To the degree you can acknowledge this and make their lives easier to create goodwill, the more likely they are to be favorable or agreeable with you.

Remember, the TAO appraisers you speak with and attempt to settle with have bosses to report to. They will rarely tell you their concerns about their boss but it is an unspoken factor.

For every case they can settle with any property owner, it is one less case they have to worry about and one less BOE hearing they have to attend. It is a win-win for everyone.

More recently, I've noticed a trend of some TAOs not willing to settle even when you do your part to reach out. Some TAOs are forcing appeals into BOE hearings because TAO representatives don't want to be the named party that grants value reductions. They would prefer to pin it on the BOE.

Unfortunately, these types of decisions are about professional self-preservation and sometimes politically motivated. There is little you can do about this except to ask why they won't settle with you.

> SETTLEMENTS REQUIRE APPROVAL

If and when you successfully negotiate a settlement with a TAO appraiser, they will provide a settlement form for you to sign.

I have seen and signed forms for different Georgia counties. Each county's settlement forms look and read very differently. So beware of this.

With every settlement form, what you are looking for is a reference to 299(c). This is short-code for Georgia Statute 48-5-299(c) that makes the 3-year tax freeze possible in Georgia when settling a tax appeal.

The objective of every negotiated settlement is to win a sufficiently lower assessed value and then freeze it for another two tax years.

It is important to know that any settlement agreement you sign with the TAO appraiser is not finalized until it is approved and signed off by the Board of Tax Assessors (BTA).

To date, I've never had any settlement agreement I signed ever get kicked back by the BTA. There is no such thing as 100% guarantee but if you sign a settlement agreement, you have a 99% chance of it being approved by the BTA. The TAO have no incentive to use more time than necessary on any single appeal.

If and when you sign any settlement agreement with the TAO

appraiser, always make sure you request the final signed copy by the BTA for your records.

> SETTLING YOUR APPEAL AT THE BOE HEARING

A trend I've noticed the last few years is the tactic of settling appeals at BOE hearings. What happens in this situation is that you and the property appraiser discuss your appeal ahead of time. Both of you come to an agreement on the value of your property. You and the appraiser then show up at the BOE hearing and tell the BOE member judges you've come to a value agreement after the opening hearing formalities.

It's been explained to me why this method is being used more by some TAOs is that the BOE helps provide cover and oversight to any settled values. Instead of the appraiser and TAO bearing the responsibility of negotiated lower values, the BOE can instead be "blamed" for lower settled values.

Instead of a signed settlement agreement between the TAO and the property owners, the paperwork comes from the BOE hearing signed off by the BOE member judges.

If this sounds like a sleight of hand way of settling appeals, it is. The point of settling appeals this way is that it gives the appearance that the BOE member judges evaluated and ruled on the appeal, not the fact that appraiser and property owner agreed to the settlement.

In my opinion, this is a political CYA tactic for TAOs. I learned through private discussions that the decision to settle cases in this manner is often made by the Chief Appraiser. It comes from the very top person at the TAO. You can expect to see more of this with more counties in the years to come.

The downside of this method of settling your appeal is that you (or your agent) may still have to appear at the BOE hearing which is still an inconvenience. However, the BOE hearing goes quicker when there is a friendly agreement between the TAO and the property owner at the outset. It saves everyone time. Everyone is happy and the appeal is resolved.

> AFTER THE SETTLEMENT

What is supposed to happen after the BTA approves your settlement with the TAO is the county's tax commissioner will send you an updated tax bill if you owe additional money. Or you will get a refund for any overpayments.

It is very rare but sometimes when the following year comes around and a new notice of assessment is issued, they list the wrong value.

In other words, the TAO goofed up and didn't freeze the value as they were supposed to. I've seen this a few times. One time, by the time we got around to sending a response, the TAO caught the mistake themselves and corrected it without our intervention. The other times, we contacted the TAO for instructions to correct it.

The bottom line is, clerical mistakes occasionally can and do happen with every TAO. It is your job to make sure the TAO doesn't make a mistake that is contrary to your interests and costs you.

> WHY YOU ARE ABLE TO "FREEZE" YOUR ASSESSED VALUES

The core of the Georgia's "property tax freeze" lies within Georgia Statute § 48-5-299(c). It has recently been revised via Georgia's H.B. 581 and became effective January 1, 2025.

(c) When the value of real property is reduced ~~or is unchanged~~ from the value on the initial annual notice of assessment or a corrected annual notice of assessment issued by the board of tax assessors and such reduced valuation has been established as the result of an appeal decision rendered by the board of equalization, hearing officer, arbitrator, or superior court pursuant to Code Section 48-5-311 or stipulated by written agreement signed by the board of tax assessors and taxpayer or taxpayer's authorized representative, the new valuation so established by appeal decision or agreement may not be increased by the board of tax assessors during the next two successive years, unless otherwise agreed in writing by both parties, subject to the following exceptions:

> *(1) This subsection shall not apply to a valuation established by an appeal decision if the taxpayer or his or her authorized repre-*

sentative failed to attend the appeal hearing or provide the board of equalization, hearing officer, or arbitrator with some written evidence supporting the taxpayer's opinion of value;

(2) This subsection shall not apply to a valuation established by an appeal decision or agreement if the taxpayer *files a return at a different valuation during the next two successive years;*

(3) Unless otherwise agreed in writing by both parties, if the taxpayer files an appeal pursuant to Code Section 48-5-311 during the next two successive years, the board of tax assessors, the board of equalization, hearing officer, or arbitrator may increase or decrease the value of the real property based on the evidence presented by the taxpayer during the appeal process; and

(4) The board of tax assessors may increase or decrease the value of the real property if, after a visual on-site inspection of the property, it is found that there have been substantial additions, deletions, or improvements to such property or that there are errors in the board of tax assessors' records as to the description or characterization of the property, or the board of tax assessors finds an occurrence of other material factors that substantially affect the current fair market value of such property.

More simply, if you attend a BOE hearing **and secure a value reduction** or you settle the appeal with the TAO **with a value reduction**, that valuation is set for the appealed year and "frozen" for the next two tax years.

I make this emphasis of **value reduction** because this is a new requirement that didn't exist prior to 2025. The good news is that there is no minimum value amount reduction specified.

Theoretically, if you ask for a $1.00 value reduction and they agree to it, you would be eligible for the 299(c) tax freeze.

I believe that the reason why the wording was changed is there was widespread abuse of obtaining the 299(c) tax freeze. Owners of multiple properties "phoned in" large numbers of tax appeals, caused a lot of unnecessary work with TAOs, and offered no legitimacy behind their appeal submissions.

If you follow the philosophy described in this book to research, compile, and submit truthful evidence for your appeals, and make good faith efforts to communicate and work with your TAO, your tax appeals are very much legitimate. You deserve to get the 299(c) tax freeze for the hard work you put into your tax appeals.

Another hypothetical scenario: you could mail in your evidence to the BOE, not show up to your hearing, and get both a value reduction and tax freeze. However, in practice, I have not yet heard this actually being done in practice.

I tell people if you want the tax freeze, try to get a settlement **with a value reduction**. And if you are unable to negotiate an acceptable settlement, then you (or someone you designate as your agent) should attend the BOE hearing to get at least a small value reduction get the 299(c) tax freeze.

However, there are some important caveats to know about the 299(c) tax freeze.

If you decide to appeal the value within those two years that would otherwise be frozen, the TAO could either increase or decrease that valuation depending on the evidence they have.

Unless you experience a substantial valuation decrease in your neighborhood or your property experiences substantial changes, damages, or deterioration, I discourage filing any appeals during the "frozen" two-year period.

Your property could later be subject to an onsite inspection. If there are substantial improvements or additions to the property that the TAO is unaware of and it substantially affects the market value of your property, the TAO could conceivably terminate the value freeze and reassess the property. The key phrase being "substantially affect the market value" which is subject to interpretation.

Bottom line, your 299(c) tax freeze is not absolute or 100% guaranteed. It is conditional. However, if you have been truthful and transparent with the information and evidence you provided with your tax appeal, you are 99% safe.

CHAPTER 9: ESCALATE YOUR APPEAL FURTHER

> APPEAL TO SUPERIOR COURT

If you are unhappy with the outcome of your BOE hearing, most people don't know they can still escalate the case further without having to pay any fees. That option is to "Appeal to Superior Court".

However, that phrase is misleading because if you decide to "Appeal to Superior Court", you actually don't go to court in the early stages. Your tax appeal goes back to the TAO to handle, not Superior Court.

This is what I consider the "fourth bite at the apple" that most property owners don't know about.

> The "first bite" is when you submit your appeal form, PT-311-A.

> The "second bite" is when you attempt to settle your case prior to a scheduled BOE hearing.

> The "third bite" is when you go through the BOE hearing.

> The "fourth bite" is at a settlement conference which occurs after you declare in writing your intentions to "Appeal to Superior Court".

It can be very confusing for property owners new to the tax appeal process. I know it was confusing for me.

I was forced to learn about this stage a few years ago when I became angry in the poor handling of one particular tax appeal by both the TAO and the BOE panel. I pursued this because "I wasn't going to take it anymore".

Anger and frustration has a way of triggering me to dig into the process further than I normally would.

In order to get a Settlement Conference, you must initiate the process, in writing, to Appeal to Superior Court. There is no way around it. You must submit a written notice within 30-days of your BOE hearing to the TAO.

Similar to the continuation letter, a written notice to appeal (now known as a petition for review) to Superior Court does not have to be long or fancy. It can be a short, one-page letter.

> SAMPLE NOTICE TO APPEAL TO SUPERIOR COURT

This is a sample template letter to "Appeal to Superior Court".

As of 2025, the verbiage in GA §48-5-311(g) was changed from "notice of appeal" to "petition for review".

In a recent conversation with a TAO in one county, I was told that, in practical terms, the "petition for review" is similar to the prior "notice of appeal".

Another county treated a "notice of appeal" the same as a "petition for review". However, you must verify with your TAO their policy on this.

In my version of the letter, I inform the TAO that I know what Settlement Conferences are. And if we cannot come to agreement, I am willing to pay the $25 filing fee to continue the appeal.

After careful thought and consideration, I submit my "Written Petition for Review" within 30 days of my BOE Hearing for the following property:

Property ID & Property Street Address here.

I understand there will be a mandatory Settlement Conference scheduled. I also understand that I may have to pay a $25 filing fee if we are unable to settle the case.

Thank you for your attention in this matter.

Sincerely,

YOUR ORIGINAL SIGNATURE
Your Name, Phone number, email address

As with the continuation letter, sign the letter with a blue-ink pen.

Generally, I recommend sending your written petition for review within two weeks of the BOE determination letter.

However, there is an exception to this suggestion. Upon the TAO's receipt of your petition for review, a settlement conference can be scheduled surprisingly quick.

Although Georgia law states that the TAO must respond to you within 45-days with a proposed meeting date and time for your Settlement Conference, they may get to back to your much quicker.

If you are unprepared, need more time, or you foresee scheduling conflicts, you may then want to postpone sending your petition for review a few more days.

However, beware. You bear responsibility for the correct counting of the 30-day deadline. The TAO will not count the days for you as in earlier steps of your appeal.

Do not cut it too close to the deadline or you might lose your right to the Settlement Conference!

As with any postal mailed letters, there is always a small risk of your notice being delayed or lost in the mail.

The TAO is supposed to use the postmark date of any delivered mail. However, I prefer these notices to arrive at the TAO well before the deadline date, whenever possible.

Because it is a one-page letter, I am comfortable with using a

First-Class postage stamp to mail it in. I will call the TAO later or visit the TAO website to confirm delivery of my letter.

Again, you have to determine your own risk-tolerance level for these types of matters.

> OVERVIEW OF SETTLEMENT CONFERENCE

Procedurally speaking, when you "Appeal to Superior Court", only the TAO is involved at the early stages. You are essentially bringing your dispute and information back to the TAO for reconsideration. That reconsideration process is called a Settlement Conference.

When your appeal goes to a Settlement Conference, you typically deal with senior, more experienced employees of the TAO. So, there are new eyes that look over your appeal with a fresh perspective.

For the TAO, the stakes are much higher especially if they cannot persuade a property owner to a settled agreement.

Unresolved appeals can become a resource-intensive situation for the TAO. They have to commit the time of senior TAO employees to cases that require a Settlement Conference.

While a Settlement Conference can be as simple as one meeting (most are), it can also be a series of communications and meetings between the property owner and TAO. It depends on the appeal and the TAO representative.

The reason why there may be several communications or meetings is that both parties need more time to resolve disagreements especially in larger property appeals.

An unresolved settlement conference in a tax appeal can be forced into the creation of a court case.

The TAO is supposed to inform the property owner they have to pay $25 filing fee within 20 days of the settlement conference to formally continue your appeal and set up a case in Superior Court.

If you choose to pay the $25 filing fee within 20 days of the settlement conference, it triggers more paperwork for the TAO.

There will likely be another wait time of 30-45 days but the TAO will assemble and submit, on your behalf, the paperwork on your appeal case and your $25 payment to Superior Court.

A superior court clerk will then assign a case number.

My Opinion on Self-Representation

In the following, I share my perspective of how things work. My information is based on a combination of personal and professional experience, research, and interviews with lawyers and other professionals from which I gained these insights.

I am not a lawyer, do not pretend to be a lawyer, and nothing you read here should be considered legal advice.

Everything in this book is for informational and educational purposes only. I do everything I can to get my information right but always remember, there are 159 counties and TAOs in Georgia.

Now that I got that out of the way, I can share my thoughts on self-representation in legal matters.

People inexperienced with civil court matters often assume that a case must go to court in front of a judge. That does not happen with most cases.

In fact, many court cases never get in front of a judge for them to rule because court cases often get settled. When court cases get settled, no one gets everything they want because everyone compromises to get a quicker final resolution.

When a civil court case is established, there are generally many tasks each party must do and prepare for prior to a court date actually being set.

Each party may have to formally exchange evidence they have so that the other side can evaluate, research, and prepare a response.

However, most of the information exchange for a tax appeal should have been done during the Settlement Conference and earlier stages. There should not be many evidentiary surprises on a tax appeal case by the time a court case has been established.

There is likely going to be renewed discussions to settle the appeal even after the $25 court filing fee is paid and a court case number has been established.

Again, there is no requirement that any court case must go in front of a judge. In fact, the chances of a tax appeal going in front of a judge is very slim even if you do pay the $25.

The TAO often rely on fear, intimidation, and "information overwhelm" to persuade you.

Many property owners have advantages they do not realize. Even if they are told about it, most property owners are too insecure or intimidated to use those advantages.

Some of this may or may not be applicable to a tax appeal court case. I am obligated to remind you to always confer with an experienced lawyer whenever possible.

One of those advantages is that many property owners own property in their personal name. As such, they are generally not required to hire a lawyer. They can self-represent their interests in a court case.

Properties in a corporate name may, at some point, require a property owner to hire a lawyer because non-lawyers are not supposed to represent corporate entities in a court case.

The TAO also has limited ability to self-represent and practice law once a court case has begun. The TAO will likely hire a lawyer to start representing them if legal motions and requests become necessary.

Hiring and employing a lawyer to represent the TAO for an extended period of time can become costly to the TAO. There is a real cost and legal expense to them.

It is certainly true that most property owners don't have legal training or legal experience to handle any court case.

But a creative, resourceful property owner can do many things that can frustrate the TAO and their lawyers. This might motivate the TAO to settle the case especially if their lawyer fees start racking up.

The reason for that is that non-lawyers that choose to self-represent are generally given wider latitude in a court case.

Contrary to popular belief, many experienced lawyers dislike having to deal with non-lawyers. They prefer to go up against other lawyers. They know the judge is likely to give every benefit of the doubt to a non-lawyer due to their inexperience and lack of legal training.

Also, due to ethical considerations, both the judge and the opposing lawyer know that they have to do their part in any court case to have a "fair fight". It is generally unethical for a trained lawyer to take "unfair legal advantage" of a non-lawyer.

In other words, the opposing lawyer has to exercise much greater care to ensure fairness to a non-lawyer than if they were going up against another trained lawyer.

There is a greater presumption of a "fair fight" when opposing parties have trained lawyers representing each party's interests.

Depending on how creative, resourceful, and knowledgeable a property owner is in self-representing, it can cost the TAO a lot of money in lawyer fees.

The primary job of any TAO is to fairly assess properties so that property taxes are paid. The end goal is to generate income for the county.

However, an overzealous TAO (or a vexatious property owner) can find themselves erasing the TAO's income. The TAO start losing money through unnecessary legal actions and legal fees.

Oftentimes, the county is best served by compromising with a property owner to settle the case. But there are overzealous employees in some TAOs who are accustomed to wielding and asserting their power.

That is why I encourage people to be strong, educated advocates for themselves. You are a property owner with appeal rights but you are also a taxpayer with taxpayer rights. There are some TAO employees that need reminding of what the big picture is and who they serve.

The TAO has to determine whether it is "worth" continuing to pay legal fees to continue moving forward with the court case.

Perhaps they should consider a settlement with the property owner so that no more resources and legal fees are spent in defending the appeal.

It can become a game of chicken in a protracted disagreement.

> MORE SETTLEMENT CONFERENCE TIPS

As I wrote earlier, a settlement conference is not always one meeting. A settlement conference can be a series of meetings and communications between the TAO and property owner.

A settlement conference ends when both the TAO and property owner come to an agreement or they mutually escalate it to Superior Court.

It is generally in the property owner's best interest to remain in the settlement conference for as long as it takes to get the results you want.

The TAO is going to probe and evaluate your position by asking you questions. They may solicit additional information and documents from you. Be professional, be respectful, but also be firm in your position if you feel it is justified.

The TAO staff are under great pressure to resolve cases quickly and efficiently if they can. But they will not offer concessions unless they know you will be resistant and you have good evidence to support your position.

Do not let the TAO staff overwhelm or intimidate you. They know most property owners are not experienced or have as much market data as they do.

They will attempt to portray themselves as being experts and more knowledgeable than you in an effort to pressure you to agree with them.

However, property owners tend to know their properties and their value better than anyone. The TAO know a lot on a macro level but not as much on the micro level of any single property.

If the TAO tries to overwhelm you with their expertise, your best response is to ask for more time or even reschedule. Time is on your side. In my view, an unsettled appeal hurts the TAO more than it does the property owner.

An unsettled appeal simply means the final amount of your final property tax bill is delayed. An unsettled appeal for the TAO means that they cannot close out the tax year.

No TAO wants to leave open a tax year for an indefinite period of time. They are accountable to the Georgia Department of Revenue. That can be used to your advantage.

The TAO may tell you that you will have to hire an attorney in the process. The truth is that there are several things a property owner can do legally **prior** to hiring a lawyer.

Many years ago, I learned there are some advantages of knowing the system well enough to be vexatious. I generally don't recommend it. But being vexatious can be persuasive against someone who refuses to be reasonable or when they are trying to take unfair advantage of you.

I won't say that all TAO staff will maliciously take unfair advantage of you and your ignorance. But it happens frequently enough. I have learned a few tricks of my own to help equalize the power imbalance. You equalize the power imbalance by understanding the process and the pressures put on the TAO.

Be prepared to let the TAO know that you are able and willing to pay the $25 filing fee if an agreement cannot be reached during the settlement conference. It is an important milestone to accept the $25 filing fee, filing appeal case paperwork, and submit it to Superior Court to process.

Many property owners believe that if they pay the $25, they automatically go to Superior Court. That is absolutely not true!

Even if you pay the $25 filing fee, the check is not deposited immediately because the TAO may not be able or want to immediately initiate a court case.

If the TAO initiates a court case, there is a high likelihood they will have to hire an attorney and start incurring that expense.

It is not uncommon for the $25 check to be held undeposited for a period of time. I presume this is intentional and the TAO wants to carefully reflect before they open the Pandora's box of starting a court case. It also takes some time to assemble the paperwork for the case.

As I said earlier, I am not a lawyer and not giving legal advice here. But I know having studied and handled various legal situations for myself, that there is always the opportunity and possibility for settlement.

Paying $25 and having a court case assigned does not mean that property owners or the TAO cannot later settle.

In fact, my research reveals that most property tax appeals that go to Superior Court often end up getting settled.

> ONCE A COURT CASE IS ESTABLISHED

You should be aware that if you paid your $25 filing fee and a court case is established, you have some decisions to make.

Keep in mind that a settlement is still possible. There are advantages to both sides to settling. However, it is also a game of chicken.

It is possible that what the TAO is offering is still unsatisfactory to you. At this point, you have one of two choices.

You can continue representing yourself and your appeal as a non-lawyer. Or you can find an experience tax appeal lawyer to represent you and your side.

There is a line in the sand where I won't speak past. It is beyond my current level of experience and expertise. It also involves a lot more knowledge about legal procedures and the legal process.

If you are unable or unwilling to settle with the TAO at this stage, this is where I must tell you to go find an experienced tax appeal lawyer to confer with.

As far as this book is concerned, this is the end of the line of pursuing a tax appeal to its process limits without the involvement of an experienced tax appeal lawyer.

However, my experience, research, and knowledge with the "Appeal to Superior Court" stage, settlement conferences, and the legal steps thereafter grows and evolves. It is an area I am actively pursuing knowledge and expertise on.

Because this late stage of tax appeals is so advanced, so few property owners reach this stage, and because of the limitations of book updates, any new information I learn about this late stage of tax appeals will be made available in a separate title, separate video, or other separate piece of work.

If and when it becomes available, you can find it on my website GeorgiaTaxAppealInfo.com.

> MAKING COMPLAINTS

In some rare instances, you may find that TAO or BOE staff or even the BOE hearing panelists may not be behaving or acting professionally. Or they might be using their innate government powers in an unfair, coercive, abusive, or threatening manner. They may become unresponsive to you. Or they might make severe mistakes that damage your rights as a taxpayer and property owner.

There can be any number of reasons where you feel that "something isn't right". In these situations, there is a "chain of command" for Georgia property tax appeals.

Like any organization, there is a management hierarchy. The larger the organization, the more difficult it is to navigate it.

In every county, the buck is supposed to stop at the Chief Appraiser. The Chief Appraiser is ultimately responsible for everything and everyone they supervise in the TAO.

If you have any complaints relating to anything within a TAO, the Chief Appraiser is where you want to address your complaint.

Some counties also have a Deputy Chief Appraiser (second-in-command) to assist the Chief Appraiser. Below the Deputy Chief Appraiser, there will be various department managers or supervisors. They can be helpful for smaller, more specific matters.

If you have a big complaint and don't want to fool around trying to find the right person, I generally recommend going straight to the Chief Appraiser.

But what happens if you don't get satisfaction with the Chief Appraiser? The next level to complain is the Board of Tax Assessors (BTA). The BTA consists of three to five members appointed by the county's governing authority.

The BTA's job is to oversee the TAO. In theory, they are part of the checks-and-balances system so that you don't have abusive, runaway TAOs. In theory, the BTA hold "public meetings".

However, very few citizens actually attend these "public meetings". If you do show up to complain, it won't be difficult to get their attention. I am very confident you will be heard.

In terms of the complaint hierarchy, if you go to the BTA to make a complaint, you can be sure the Chief Appraiser will know about it. The Chief Appraiser reports to and is accountable to the BTA.

In many counties, especially smaller ones, members of the BTA and Chief Appraiser and the TAO can be tight-knit. You might feel that complaining to the BTA against a Chief Appraiser might feel awkward. I know I have contemplated this scenario myself.

In this situation, if I felt really motivated and aggrieved, I would then complain to the Georgia Department of Revenue.

Ultimately, the BTA, the BOE panelists, and the entire TAO operation of property valuations falls under the purview of the Georgia Department of Revenue.

Hopefully, you will never have to complain about something fishy, unprofessional, or abusive. But if you do, you now have a general roadmap for your complaint.

CONCLUSION

I Want To Hear From You!

Allow me to personally thank you for your purchase. I would love to hear your comments and feedback.

It is my intention to update this book at least once a year. It could be more frequent depending on the feedback and comments I receive.

If you are an Amazon Kindle eBook customer, you will automatically receive book updates free of charge through the Amazon Kindle system.

Do you have a success story with your appeal?
Did you get a substantial value reduction?
Did you successfully negotiate a settlement?
Did you get your tax freeze?
Did you encounter glitches or setbacks in your appeal?
Did you find errors that I missed?
Did you find any information to be incorrect?
Did you encounter a situation or scenario I didn't cover?
Is there anything in this book that I could have done better?
What can I do to improve this book?

Send me an email to: ***MattRealty1@gmail.com***.

When you send me email, make sure you provide your name and the county you are in.

If I am deserving, please leave me a 5-star book review rating on

Amazon.

It would really help me a lot and help ensure that I continue my work for property owners and the public for years to come.

Thank you for reading!

Matthew S. Chan, MBA
Real Estate Broker/Instructor/Investor
Georgia R.E. License: #391253
Georgia R.E. Instructor: #435531
MattRealty1@gmail.com

P.S. Visit & Subscribe to my YouTube channel, **Tax Freeze Command**.

The direct link to my channel is:
http://youtube.com/@TaxFreezeCommand.

ADDITIONAL RESOURCES

If you are a Georgia real estate agent or real estate broker, I offer a class on Georgia Tax Appeals for CE credit through my real estate school, Intrepid Real Estate Education. The website is http://RealEstateEducation1.com. I offer both live and virtual CE classes.

If you are a homeowner, landlord, or real estate investor who want additional information or training on Georgia tax appeals, I will be offering a self-paced, video Master Course and other titles in the near future.

They will go into more detail, give more nuance, live examples, special situations, case studies, and private/personal stories I can't cover in this book.

Send an email to **MattRealty1@gmail.com** and I will keep you in the loop. Future announcements will also be published on my website: GeorgiaTaxAppealInfo.com. The website is http://GeorgiaTaxAppealinfo.com.

Every month, I make new videos on Georgia property tax appeals on my YouTube channel, **Tax Freeze Command**.

http://youtube.com/@TaxFreezeCommand.

Visit and SUBSCRIBE to keep up-to-date.

ABOUT THE AUTHOR

Matthew S. Chan is a licensed Real Estate Broker & Instructor in Georgia and Florida. Prior to becoming a Real Estate Broker, Matthew was a real estate investor/principal of 20 years who bought, sold, financed, and leased properties in Georgia and Alabama.

Matthew is also well-versed in property tax appeal matters and has represented and negotiated 250+ tax appeals across six Georgia counties. To date, Matthew has earned 1,100+ hours of Real Estate CE Credits from over two dozen real estate schools.

In publishing, Matthew is the publisher and author of "The Turn-Key Investor" series of books, manuals, and audio programs.

Over his career as a facilitator and instructor, Matthew has taught and lead real estate/entrepreneur meetings, classes, seminars, and workshops both in the U.S. and internationally.

Matthew has served as adjunct instructor/professor at these academic institutions:

- Seminole State College
- Valencia College
- Trident Technical College (Continuing Education)

Prior to his career in real estate, Matthew worked in the I.T. industry as a network administrator and network engineer. He advanced to become a national technical trainer teaching networking courses throughout the U.S. and even in Europe.

Matthew's formal education includes a Bachelor of Science in Business Administration (BSBA) from University of Central Florida and a Masters of Business Administration (MBA) from Webster University.

Matthew is also a YouTuber and hosts the **"Tax Freeze Command"** YouTube channel.

REFERENCES

Chatham County Board of Assessors

Cobb County Board of Tax Assessors

DeKalb County Property Appraisal

Fulton County Board of Assessors

Georgia Department of Revenue

Gwinnett County Tax Assessors

Macon-Bibb County Board of Tax Assessors

Muscogee County Board of Tax Assessors

Augusta-Richmond Board of Assessors

END OF BOOK

Remember, if you are a Kindle book customer, this book will be updated periodically. Don't forget to refresh your Amazon Kindle reader annually.

The end... for now.

Proof of Purchase Answer

The names of my cats are: Lexy and Jaggy. :-)

Made in the USA
Monee, IL
04 November 2026

67387243R00085